SEXUAL CHARACTER

SEXUAL CHARACTER

Beyond Technique to Intimacy

Marva J. Dawn

WILLIAM B. EERDMANS PUBLISHING COMPANY
GRAND RAPIDS, MICHIGAN

Copyright © 1993 by Wm. B. Eerdmans Publishing Co.
255 Jefferson Ave. S.E., Grand Rapids, Michigan 49503

Printed in the United States of America

Reprinted 1999

Library of Congress Cataloging-in-Publication Data

Dawn, Marva J.
   Sexual character: beyond technique to intimacy /
Marva J. Dawn.
      p.   cm.
   Includes bibliographical references.
   ISBN 0-8028-0700-3 (paper)
   1. Sex — Religious aspects — Christianity. 2. Sexual ethics.
3. Character. I. Title.
BT708.D385   1993
241'.66 — dc20
                               93-1216
                               CIP

The author and publisher gratefully acknowledge permission to
reprint the poem by Mark Littleton found on pp. 39 and 40.

This book is dedicated to

those tired of the emptiness of chasing from one sexual experience to another;

youth confused by the sexual promiscuity of our society;

parents wondering how to talk with their kids about "sex";

spouses longing to be more faithful;

spouses wanting to make sure their marriage is secure;

singles yearning for the courage to remain celibate;

pastors needing tools for counseling young members of the
congregation;

all of us seeking God's guidance for living truthfully;

the Church, so that it can offer the world alternative models of
friendship and covenant marriage and Joy-full sexuality;

and especially to Myron, most precious treasure, whose loving
faithfulness in spite of my physical handicaps is truly a
great mystery.

CONTENTS

CONTENTS

ACKNOWLEDGMENTS

This book is not written presumptuously, as if I thought myself capable of work superior to previous analyses of sexual ethics. Rather, this book is built upon the insights and expertise of countless others — primarily the numerous youth and adults who have given me feedback in seminars on sexuality at churches, camps, and high schools. For example, Evelyn Jeppeson (of blessed memory) reminded me to speak against the flippancy of our culture's use of the word *sex,* and Angela Vahsholtz pointed me to a helpful magazine piece on abortion. Most of all, this book simply expounds the truths of the Hebrew and Christian Scriptures.

I am profoundly grateful to three theologians for their gifts to this book. Both analysis and response are critical elements in Christian ethics. Jacques Ellul provided much of the background analysis of culture through my dissertation project on his works. Walter Brueggemann has been a great inspiration to me because of his emphasis on faithful biblical interpretation and obedience as the response. Stanley Hauerwas first taught me about "Ethics of Character" during my graduate program at Notre Dame. He will probably wish upon reading this that I had learned more from him, but he moved to Duke after my first year. I will never stop learning from his books and presentations.

I especially want to thank Karyl Groeneveld, whose far better eyes and vastly superior skills make her an invaluable resource for Hebrew exegetical work. With great mastery, she continues to scrutinize texts for me in spite of severe chronic pain and kindly facilitates my study for lectures and books by printing all the results of her thorough labor in large type.

Michael and Karen Dismer read the second draft of the manuscript and gave helpful suggestions. More important, they provided the enfolding of Christian community during all my single years and now continue to encourage my teaching and writing with the profound gift of their loving friendship.

Because of my limited vision I could not get along without Yvonne Mettler, who proofread the final manuscript with me. Also, I am very grateful to Jennifer Hoffman, my editor at Eerdmans, with whom it is a pleasure to work.

My parents, Louise and Herold Gersmehl, deserve the greatest thanks for the wonderful model they have been throughout my life of persons both pursuing God's purposes for their life together and also having the courage to make our home an alternative community.

INTRODUCTION

I have stewed about this book in an overabundance of doctors' offices, waiting rooms, and emergency clinics. In the midst of profound physical pain and frustration over our inability to deal adequately with the ravages of debilitating chronic disease, I have had enormous opportunities to contemplate the profound spiritual pain and emotional/social frustration that lie at the root of sexual behavior in the United States.

My basic presuppositions will be very obvious in the pages that follow, but I declare them gladly. First of all, much of my thinking depends upon the belief that human beings are coherent creatures. What we do with our bodies is integrally related to what is developing in our minds, our emotions, and the innermost core that is truly who we are — our spirits and souls.[1]

Second, I am convinced — by logic, experience, history,

---

1. Although I thoroughly disagree with her understanding of the meaning of, and the appropriate framework for, sexual intercourse, the total integration of sexual experience and spirituality is demonstrated by Joan H. Timmerman's *Sexuality and Spiritual Growth* (New York: Crossroad, 1992).

and faith — that the truths of Christianity include accurate, workable, and delightful visions and guidelines for human sexuality. I believe that the Bible is inspired by the Holy Spirit, that God got what God wanted in the Scriptures, in spite of the human authors and editors he[2] used and the literary forms they fashioned to convey his revelation to humankind.

Third, I think that yet another book on sexual ethics IS critically necessary because we live in desperate times and because much of the analysis has been inadequate. Present sexual behavior and family structures in the United States are leading to escalations of sexually transmitted diseases and sexual violence and to decreased well-being for children in our society. Something radical must be done — and I use the word *radical* to emphasize getting to the roots of the problems. Consider the urgency of the need. The Children's Defense Fund Report of May 1988 quotes the following statistics of occurrences *in one day* in the life of United States children and teenagers:

2,753 get pregnant;
1,099 have abortions;
  367 miscarry;
1,287 give birth;
7,742 become sexually active;
  609 get syphilis or gonorrhea;
1,868 drop out of school;
3,288 run away from home;
1,736 are in adult jails;

2. Out of my concern to reach the widest audience possible, I have chosen to refer to God with the masculine pronouns *he, his,* and *him.* I recognize that these pronouns are inadequate, for God is neither male nor female, but more than all our words can ever connote. I apologize to anyone who might be offended by my word choices and pray that you will accept my decision to use our inadequate language as carefully as possible for many kinds of people.

The "pain" of our sexual confusion

2,989 experience the breakup of the family
through divorce.

And these are statistics for 1988! What must they be now?
I believe that the Christian Church could lead the way in
offering better alternatives for contemporary life-styles.

Most recently in an emergency room I waited as a
doctor tried to ascertain if the almost unbearable pain in
my head was related to increased retinal hemorrhaging in
my eye. The situation gave birth to a three-part analogy
between physical and sexual behaviors. When we have a
physical pain, we take something to ease it. But to deal
only with the symptoms is inadequate. We must find the
source of the pain. And then we must do something about
the true reason for our pain.

e.g.

It can be readily seen that much of the sexual behavior
in U.S. society arises subconsciously as the initial effort to
cope with inexplicable pain. But we must diagnose the
situation more accurately and determine the true source of
that pain. And then we can find remedies for our society's
ills, possibilities for sexual expression, and hope for sexual
fulfillment.

My initial statements in this introduction perhaps
sound elementary, but in various sexual behavior workshops with teens and adults around the country I have
discovered that the elementary principles are rarely enun-
ciated. Young people often say to me, "No one has ever
told me this before," and adults frequently lament, "If only
someone had told me these things sooner, I could have
spared myself a lot of pain."

The basic principles need to be affirmed and ex-
pounded. Who are we as human beings? What is the nature
of our sexuality? What forces in our society contribute to
present understandings of sexuality and its genital expression? How does our Christian faith relate to all of this?

Please explore these issues with me. The need in our

xiii

society for better understanding of our sexuality is critical, so we cannot waste any time. If my thinking is unclear or wrong, please correct me. If you find what is written here to be helpful, pass it on to every family, pastor, and others you know. Discuss it in youth groups, junior high Sunday school classes, adult forums, singles groups, and clergy conferences. This is an urgent matter. Let us help our world to discover genuine sexual freedom and delight!

MARVA J. DAWN
REFORMATION DAY, 1992

I *The Basis for New Thinking about Our Sexuality*

For whoever is in Christ, there IS a new creation.

2 CORINTHIANS 5:17

Therefore . . . present yourselves to God as those alive from the dead and the aspects of your body as instruments of righteousness to God.

ROMANS 6:13

1 Our Society's Pain and Its Sexual Coping

The Ache of our Confusion

We do not need statistics. You can read them every-where — in books and journals, in reports of commissions and task forces, in church documents and educational materials. We are shocked by numbers such as those of the Children's Defense Fund Report cited in the Introduction. Such statistics give us a level of thought that immobilizes us. We can't handle the thought that 7,742 youth in the United States become sexually active each day, so we don't do anything at all. Statistics are one aspect of the technological milieu (explored more thoroughly in the next chapter) causing the very problems we are investigating; therefore, to fill this book with statistics would be counterproductive.

On the other extreme, we do not need cosmic abstractions. We need a median level of perception, a broad sweep of the forest that does not get bogged down in individual trees. This chapter simply sketches some of the colors that compose the whole picture of sexual behavior in the United States and the effects of that milieu. We will realize that much of the behavior chosen to relieve our society's sexual ache actually increases the pain instead.

3

The Overtness of Genital Sexuality in Our Milieu

No one will deny that genital sexuality continues to be expressed more and more overtly in the United States; we need only compare contemporary television programs with those we saw as children. My husband Myron and I recently were pleasantly reminded by the fifty-year-old movie *Casablanca* of how genteel and discreet the portrayal of romance was half a century ago. Myron noted that all great literature, such as Shakespeare's, is similarly more subtle. "Alfred Hitchcock movies, for example, are much more scary," he remarked, "because you rarely see all the blood and gore. You don't see people getting hacked up with chainsaws." Because our society has lost the meaning of mystery and sexuality and misunderstands this inverse proportion, violence must be displayed more and more severely and sexual expression has to become more and more explicit to excite. Human nature requires a continuous escalation of stimulation, especially if the scintillation itself is the only meaning that remains.

We see, hear, and feel the effects of this escalating explicitness everywhere — outrageously graphic promotion of sexual violence in rock music and rap, sexy models advertising all kinds of products, jokes about the local prostitution associated with military bases, condom distribution in schools, television sitcoms with many young characters asking for birth control, sleeping together, or pregnant. Overtness about genital sexuality even invades the political sphere. As one national news magazine lamented in the fall of 1992,

> Today, we are bombarded with the most intimate details of our leaders' lives — topped by the spectacle of one presidential candidate discussing his troubled marriage on national television and the other candidate denying rumors of infidelity.

4

Just as the news article concluded, we must also ask, "When intimacy is thrust upon us, does it lose its value?"[1] When our senses are so bombarded by explicit sexual behavior, when our social milieu is so saturated with sexual innuendoes, we must be driven to urgent questions about this loss of meaning.

Adult Sexual Behavior

Basically, the assumption in our society is that genital sexual expression is the "be-all and end-all" of human existence. Persons deserve sexual pleasure, they must have it, and — no matter what — they *will* have it.

What attitudes, behaviors, and results does such an assumption generate? On the one hand, peer pressure teaches teenagers that they must "score" on the first date. On the other hand, men express confusion about how to court a woman without it being perceived as harassment. Singles are ridiculed if they remain virgins; others wonder how to ask the right questions so they won't risk having sexual intercourse with an unsafe partner. Militant gays and lesbians disrupt worship services to demand that churches accept their unions; the behavior of child molesters is sometimes driven by homophobic fears.

Meanwhile, rapes and parental sexual abuse are increasing and are increasingly reported. The incidence of sexually transmitted diseases is on the rise. Half the marriages in the United States end in divorce — often as one or both spouses turn to a new, more exciting sexual partner. Yet a *U.S. News and World Report* Science and Society feature on "Sexual Desire" begins with the large-print caption,

1. Steven V. Roberts, "Looking for the Light in Their Souls," *U.S. News and World Report* 113, 9 (31 Aug.–7 Sept. 1992): 15.

"Whether it's dull appetite or ravenous hunger, millions of Americans are unhappy with their intimate lives."[2]

Many live with several different partners in succession or live together to see if marriage will work. However, on the basis of a twenty-three-year research project, sociologists William G. Axinn of the University of Chicago and Arland Thornton of the University of Michigan concluded that "cohabitation weakens commitment to marriage." Their research showed that the experience of setting up unmarried households "produces attitudes and values which increase the probability of divorce." Other studies show that divorce rates among those who have previously lived together are fifty to one hundred percent higher.[3]

Sexual therapists and psychologists counsel millions who are dissatisfied with sexual experiences or struggling to find stability and permanence in relationships. People yearn for fulfillment and meaning in their sexual lives.

The Effects of this Milieu on Children

Most distressing are the effects of this sexually explicit milieu on the children of our society. A social worker/counselor recently informed me that it is now estimated that one-third of females and one-sixth of males in the United States have experienced sexual harassment; twenty percent of the victimizers are teenagers.

Suffering abuse themselves, bombarded by media, or exposed to the sexual confusions and behaviors of their parents, children become sexually active at earlier ages.

2. Lynn Roselinni, "Sexual Desire," *U.S. News and World Report* 113, 1 (6 July 1992): 60-66.
3. "Living Together Might Weaken Marriage Commitment," Associated Press report, *The Columbian* (Vancouver, WA), 3 Sept. 1992.

Students in Myron's third-grade classroom use sexual language that we never even heard, much less uttered, when we were in high school.

A large percentage of children live in single-parent homes, are shuffled between two sets of parents, or are raised by grandparents — and wonder about the possibility of security and stability. They observe their parent's adultery or fornication and wonder about the meaning of sexual union.

The nature of our society is starkly revealed by the very important questions young people ask. At the end of a Christian college forum outlining God's design for our sexuality (as will be presented in this book), a student asked me, "What if you save sex for marriage and then it isn't good?"

We must explore what that student meant by "good." Our society looks for "good sex" as a relief for its soul-suffering, but prevalent sexual behaviors don't come close to touching the profound pain. Those of us who care had better take our world to the emergency room and find the true source of its pain.

2 The True Source of the Pain

Absence of Intimacy

During one of the loneliest periods of my many single years, I found myself faced with a very inviting possibility for an affair. As I wrestled within myself — debating between the side of me that wanted to be faithful to my previous deliberate choice of celibacy and the side of me that wanted to rebel against that constantly careful self-discipline — I tested my thoughts by opening up the issue with a close Christian friend.

After I lamented how lonely I was and how wonderfully comforting the possible affair seemed, Dan responded, "I want to be here for you when you come back." I asked what he meant, and he continued, "If you have an affair, you will regret it. I want to help pick up the pieces when you hate yourself."

Good heavens! If my Christian brother loves me like that, who needs an affair?

What I truly needed at that point was not genital experimentation, but the security and comfort of knowing experientially that someone genuinely cared about me. I needed to know that I was not alone in my pain.

On the other hand, one of my best friends has chosen

otherwise. She moved in with her boyfriend and threw out her devotional practices, her life's focus, her faith. One major difference underneath our choices is that she did not have a genuinely supportive Christian community to surround her in her loneliness. In fact, a primary reason for what she calls her "necessary rebellion" was the tragedy that the Christian organization in which she had worked had failed miserably to be Christian.

It seems to me that much of the sexual behavior in U.S. society today is grounded in the failure to distinguish between our profound needs for support on the level of social sexuality and the attraction of exciting genital stimulation. Moreover, the genuine needs in the realm of social sexuality are heightened by the non-intimacy of a technological milieu. Finally, underneath these contemporary problems is a universal and timeless spiritual problem, for sexual expression has become a major form of idolatry in our culture.

The Distinction Between Social and Genital Sexuality

Everyday observations of teenagers, single adults, and parents at college campuses, counseling sessions, and retreats (which could readily be undergirded with psychological clinical analysis of human behavior and sociological data about social patterns) have led to the conclusion that the sexual behavior of many persons arises because of our society's confusion between social and genital sexuality.[1] Biblically, the two kinds of sexuality are introduced in Genesis 1 and 2.

1. These terms for this distinction came from Joyce Huggett's *Dating, Sex, and Friendship* (Downers Grove, IL: InterVarsity Press, 1985).

Genesis 2 especially underscores the whole scriptural presentation of God's design for genital sexuality (to be explicated more thoroughly in the following chapter and in Part II of this book). In Genesis 2:24 the man is commanded to leave his father and mother and cleave to his wife (a most amazing ordinance in contrast to a patriarchal society!). The result is a new family unit and unity, especially marked by the covenantal sign of genital union.

Quite distinctly, Genesis 1:26-27 proclaims liturgically the creation of human beings as the culmination of God's sovereign, harmonious ordering of the world. Human beings are especially created to image God, and a significant part of that imaging is fellowship.[2] In our relationships with each other, we model the community of the Trinity.

Moreover, we discover our own personal sexuality in the ways we image aspects of God's character. This combats the problem of culturally stereotyped roles. My parents encouraged my deepest enjoyments and set me free as a child to discover my particular femininity in playing football and every other kind of ball imaginable. That childhood experience enabled me in my early career to develop possibilities for serving the Church as a female even though I had grown up in a denomination that had previously limited the theological realm entirely to men. But this is who I am, and at that time it did not make me any less feminine to display God's character through attributes and work styles and subject or project choices formerly thought to be masculine.

It seems almost silly to write that paragraph in these days when society pretends to open all roles to women — and yet I think it is necessary because our culture suffers from a great confusion over what constitutes masculinity and femininity. I do not intend to solve that problem in this

2. See Paul K. Jewett, *Man as Male and Female* (Grand Rapids: William B. Eerdmans, 1975).

book, but I must point out that it is extremely helpful (though not at all sufficient) for Christian persons to define their masculinity and femininity in terms of how we each image God in our unique personalities and particular social sexuality.

Jesus gives us the perfect model for social sexuality. His gentleness and concern for the marginalized smash the stupid stereotypes of male machismo. His strength and courage overturn the sticky sentimental notions of "Jesus meek and mild." He kept his social sexuality distinct from his genital sexuality by relating in powerfully wholesome, upbuilding, nongenital ways with persons of both sexes. Frequently his support for "naughty women" set them free to "go and sin no more" genitally.

Our social sexuality is composed of all aspects of our being that are distinct from specific feelings, attitudes, or behaviors related or leading to genital union. When I speak with you, I do not do so as a neuter. I relate to you as a woman, with my particular body and spirit and mind, with my whole self, which has discovered its identity within the framework of my being female. How I relate to everyone else in the world in every kind of human interaction depends upon the way in which my social sexuality has been formed. I write, teach, buy groceries, or talk with someone on an airplane out of my social sexuality. Also, in my own unique personality, in social situations I express a woman's affection in many ways — hugs, touches, kisses, words — but these are carefully chosen to be fully loving and honorable, thoroughly reserving all expressions of genital sexuality for one and only one person, my husband.

In order to preserve this distinction between genital and social sexuality, we need complete support of our personal identities. Without affection, approval, and the knowledge that one belongs in some sort of community, a person might become desperate and falsely assume that what is needed is genital sexual expression rather than social affection. Donald

Joy asks, "Who's Holding Your Trampoline?" and calls for support from family, extended family, friends, and colleagues.[3] Just as all four sides of a trampoline must be firmly supported or the one bouncing on it will crash, so our personal selfhood must be thoroughly supported by the people who surround us. If the fundamental groups of people that Dr. Joy mentions do not affirm us, we need to find alternative means of support.

I am convinced that, if the Church could provide more thorough affection and care for persons, many would be less likely to turn falsely to genital sexual expression for the social support they need. However, the Church must learn to be more deliberately intentional about forming community[4] because of the nature of the milieu in which we live. Part of the reason why many persons in our society don't experience adequate support for their social sexuality is that various aspects of our technological milieu destroy intimacy or hinder its development.

The Lack of Intimacy
in a Technological Milieu

Primarily my thesis in this chapter is built from the social insights of Jacques Ellul,[5] who has demonstrated for more

3. Donald M. Joy, *Bonding: Relationships in the Image of God* (Waco, TX: Word Books, 1985), pp. 3-13.

4. My book *The Hilarity of Community: Romans 12 and How to Be the Church* (Grand Rapids: William B. Eerdmans, 1992) is designed with study questions to help develop deeper relationships in Christian congregations; see especially chapters 18 and 19.

5. Because Ellul's comments about sexuality and the technological milieu are scattered throughout his extensive corpus in social criticism and Christian ethics, specific ideas will not be footnoted in this book, though a list of the most important sources can be found in the bibliography. For detailed footnoting and exposition of his ideas, see Marva J. Dawn, "The Concept of 'The Principalities and

than forty-five years the devastating effects of a technological society on human experience. In contrast, for most of the history of human beings their milieu was that of their social grouping. Individuals functioned within tribes or clans to find ways to tame nature or combat enemies.

The following illustration is meant not to be universal, nor to be too reductionistic, but merely to illustrate the kinds of changes that have happened in the social fabric of the United States. Consider a family which in previous eras might have been a cohesive unit, with all the family members working together on the family farm or in the family cobbler shop. Not only were the individual members knit together by their blood ties, but they also spent much of their time together, shared common economic/political goals, and suffered common social/psychological/physical strains. This structure might not have been particularly harmonious, but at least the underlying skeleton of the situation fostered some cohesion among family members.

This basic social fabric began to unravel with the onset of the Industrial Revolution. Now instead of working together with family members in their own shop, the father of the household went to a factory for his work. Not only were the family members not together during the day and sharing in the same economic endeavor, but also the father brought home the particular psychological stresses of the factory to add to the mix of the family's own emotional strains. When World War II took women into factories also to work for pay, the pressures on the family unit were multiplied severalfold. Now, not only were spouses not together physically, emotionally, and economically, but also both husband and wife brought home the particular strains of their jobs and work environments. When the children started working at fast-food outlets, the strains were multiplied again.

Powers' in the Works of Jacques Ellul" (Ph.D. diss., University of Notre Dame, 1992).

Even more drastic changes in the social fabric occurred with the rise of the technological society and its conspicuous consumption. Values have shifted so that in some families children are considered an economic liability rather than a boon. If the only value that is held by the family cohesively is consumption, then children too young to work do not contribute to the family's well-being.

Moreover, in the technological society the various toys and tools of the milieu pull persons away from intimacy. Think of some of the specifics in your own life. For example, my childhood family sometimes played games together. Now many families simply watch television[6] — or, even worse, family members watch different programs on personal televisions in separate rooms. My brothers and I did dishes together — and often sang together as we worked. Now in most households one person puts the dishes into the dishwasher.

Children used to imitate their parents at work. Boys had little milking stools and accompanied their fathers to the barn. Girls had miniature rolling pins and baking pans, from which they graduated to increased participation in the actual family baking. These shared activities gave opportunities for conversation and affectionate intimacy. Of course, the possibility doesn't imply its fulfillment, but remember that we are only painting here a broad portrait of the basic social fabric.

In a technological milieu, children are less able to imitate their parents' jobs. They imitate instead their leisure activities, many of which have become solo endeavors — watching television or movies, riding on sports vehicles, playing video games. One doesn't even need a partner anymore to play chess — the computer is more challenging.

6. For a frightening report on the way in which too much television watching destroys language skills and reduces the size of a person's brain, see Jane M. Healy, *Endangered Minds: Why Our Children Don't Think* (New York: Simon and Schuster, 1990).

Many years ago when I led youth retreats, I could build rapport with some of the kids and gather illustrations for Bible studies by all the fun (jokes and sharing snacks and sometimes serious talk) we would have in the car on the way to the camp. Now frequently there is no conversation in the vehicle at all if all of the youth plug Walkmans in their ears and go off to their own private worlds.

The effects of Walkmans and musical videos are especially evident in the singing of young people. Formerly it was easy to get youth to participate in singing at a retreat, but now they are more accustomed to being observers, listeners, often singing only vicariously through the input of their earplugs. Fewer children know the basics of music or can read musical scores. In contrast, my father's former seventh- and eighth-grade choirs sang in four-part harmony!

The isolation of youth in our society and the false intimacy created by the fabricated relationships of a technological milieu are thoroughly displayed by the knowledgeable multiple authors of *Dancing in the Dark: Youth, Popular Culture, and the Electronic Media*. An extremely disturbing chapter, "Rocking to Images: The Music Television Revolution," exposes this deception:

> By directly manipulating human emotion while hiding their strings, by creating an appealing, impressionistic mood that devalues logical analysis and rational critique, MTV gives young viewers what they want without clarifying what it is they get.[7]

The company's chairman Bob Pittman callously asserts, "At MTV, we don't shoot for the 14-year-olds, we own them."[7]

---

7. Quentin J. Schultze et al., *Dancing in the Dark: Youth, Popular Culture, and the Electronic Media* (Grand Rapids: William B. Eerdmans, 1991), p. 204.

8. Schultze et al., *Dancing in the Dark*, p. 192.

These are just a few examples of the ways in which our technological toys and propaganda control us, pull us away from each other, make us less inclined to participate with the group, cause us to be less capable of interactions with others. Similarly, our technological tools decrease our skills for intimacy.

In all of my descriptions it is important to remember that I am not opposed to technology per se. Its tools are wonderfully helpful — but we must clearly see the ways in which they work to lessen our humanity. For example, computers are powerful time-savers. They make book writing much easier since I don't have to type eight or ten drafts of a manuscript. I can do my revisions on the screen and print as often as necessary without having to retype. But my interactions with others will be lessened if I only send them messages through the computer modem. Even a telephone call is less intimate than being with friends and talking together face-to-face.

There is no going back to an earlier era. We live in the technological society and can use its tools and toys to our advantage. But we must always be aware of the ways in which these technological advances pull us away from each other. In the particular concern of this book for sexual ethics, we must understand that the desperation in our society for intimacy often leads to genital experimentation by those who truly long instead for social affection.

Jacques Ellul brilliantly recognizes that the present state of our milieu causes us to reverse the poles of intimacy and technology. Because deep inside we know that our lives are less intimate, we try to create that intimacy, but we don't know how to do it in any other ways than through technique. For example, sexual union, which is most satisfying as the culminating expression of growing intimacy in many human dimensions, has been ripped out of that context and placed as the initiating act for relationships. Since it then has no corresponding intimacies, improvements must deal with the very act itself, and consequently we have to write manuals on techniques to make "sex" more exciting. This is the wrong remedy for our emotional aches; the true source of the pain has not been diagnosed.

On the other hand, we intimize our technology. We advertise our technological toys and tools with sexy models or cozy images designed to make them appear less sterile. For example, the telephone advertisement "Reach out and touch someone" is one of the most deceiving of all illusions. It makes us feel cozy about our communications and hides from us the fact that our need to telephone each other arises because we do not live close enough or we are too busy to spend time together. The telephone is certainly a wonderful tool, but it must always be recognized as second best. (I am grateful to be able to hear my husband's voice when I am away on a teaching trip, but I would much rather have his hug in person.) Friendships and family relationships require quality time together for intimacy to thrive.

The point of this whole section is that the very nature of a technological milieu prevents our social fabric from being conducive to the development of intimacy. A friend of mine who teaches in a Christian school asked her students how their parents tucked them in at night. One boy nonchalantly answered, "Oh, my parents don't tuck me in. They just say good-night over the intercom." We are shocked — at least we should be if we care about the nurturing of children.

To whom will this boy turn in his future search for affection? Will he find support in friends and colleagues and others to hold up his trampoline? Or will he falsely turn his desire to sexual conquest, with the same kind of indifference demonstrated by his parents?

The Idolatry of "Sex"
in Contemporary Society

Throughout history, basic sexual desire has caused human beings to turn the need for affection and genital sexual expression into a god. Also, our fundamental, intense longing for intimacy with God — part of the "eternity" in our soul — is misunderstood as yearning for human intimacy. It isn't new that in our present epoch "sex" should be one of the major idolatries.

What is new is the present foundation of this idolatry: the severity of non-intimacy in a technological milieu and the desperation of people to fill the void, coupled with the decrease in skills and opportunities for wholesome affection and a growing inability to distinguish between social and genital sexuality. These factors cause the idolatry to be particularly intense and, contrarily, less noticed for the idolatry that it really is.

This subtlety startled me in the midst of a retreat, during a conversation in which celibacy for both homosexuals and single heterosexuals was advocated. A woman exclaimed, "Why should certain groups of people be denied the possibility for sexual expression? That's not fair." The implication in the ensuing discussion was that persons who were denied sexual expression would be less than human. I thought of my quadriplegic friend Linden's remark that he is still sexual and human even if he is not capable of feeling genital sexual pleasure.

What constitutes our humanity? Is physical, sensual pleasure essential for quality of life? Is genital sexual expression the most important element of our existence? Our society seems to say that it is. The idolatry is so pervasive that we rarely notice how much it infects rational discussion.

Another illustration of the ubiquity of the idolatry is our perception of affection. A friend of mine commented upon her observation in Italy of same-gender friends walking hand in hand down the street. She remarked that if we saw that in our society, we would probably immediately assume that it indicated homosexuality. The idolatry of genital sexuality and the failure to distinguish it from social sexuality has made it impossible for friends to express affection without being misunderstood.

As the rise of the technological milieu has de-intimized our society, the growing desperation for intimacy leads to an ever greater frenzy about genital sexual expression. Many persons caught in these social attitudes about sexual satisfaction find only emptiness and are therefore searching for alternatives.

What does our Christian faith have to say to all of this? What kinds of alternatives can the Christian community offer to the sexual understandings and behaviors of our society?

19

3 A Genuine Remedy —
"Sex Is Like a Typewriter!"

I hope that the title of this chapter makes you uncomfortable. We should dislike the flippancy with which our culture talks about "sex," for language influences our character. Whereas some persons in our society might chase after "sex," God's people search for his design for "sexual union," a permanent relationship rather than a fleeting experience. More important, we should resist the notion that something so beautiful and deeply expressive as sexual union should be likened to something so cold and sterile — so technologically non-intimate — as a typewriter.

Like all analogies, this one fails drastically in every other aspect besides the point it is intended to make. The analogy that "sex is like a typewriter" is useful only in the way it directs us to the true remedy for our inexplicable pain.

"Sex Is Like My Typewriter"

Before the personal computer era, I used an excellent typewriter to write books. It had a corrector ribbon that was especially helpful — except that I didn't have to change it often enough to remember how to do it. Besides, the corrector and typing ribbons had to be carefully positioned around certain sprockets and divider bars in order not to interfere with each other's functioning. In addition, my vision had already partially deteriorated, and, most important, I have always been a total klutz mechanically. Consequently, every time the corrector ribbon had to be changed I wound up with inky hands and a nonfunctioning machine.

Then the most amazing thing always happened: I would get out the instruction book. A picture showed me how the ribbons were to be positioned, and written instructions guided me step by step through the process of threading them into place. Voila! I could successfully type and correct!

Why could that instruction book solve my problem every time? It is because the company that built the typewriter wrote the instruction book. Those who know the design of the machine are the ones most able to teach me how the machine can be most effectively used and maintained.

That is how our sexuality is like my typewriter. The Designer knows the design and is the best one to write the instruction book. God, who created us in the wholistic unity of our bodies, souls, minds, and spirits, made our sexuality part of that wholeness and integrally related to every other aspect of our beings. God also graciously revealed his design for the care of our sexuality in the Scriptures. Just as with my typewriter, if we fail to follow the Designer's instructions and handle our sexuality our own way — or the way our society teaches us — we wind up with messy hands and a nonfunctioning instrument. But if we follow the Creator's instructions, the instrument works effectively, productively, delightfully. Its purpose is fulfilled.

God designed us for relationships with others, for social affection and caring in fellowship with everyone else.

Specifically, he designed sexual intercourse as a special sign of a unique relationship, one that develops out of leaving former family bonds and cleaving to one and only one person for the rest of our lives. What a beautiful design! It creates the possibility for a mysterious love, for human security and stability, for confidence and trust, for the welcoming of children into the world, and for nurturing them into well-being by holding up the trampoline of their social sexuality. Then they, too, will have the strength of character faithfully to reserve their genital sexuality for this precious gift of permanent commitment.

I can only write this chapter because I am a Christian. In general, the modern mind-set rejects the idea of a transcendent God, an Absolute, the belief that there is an order, a design, a supernatural realm beyond the material with which we deal, an ultimate meaning in life.[1] That is why it is critically urgent that we who believe in a Creator offer the alternatives of our understanding to those who have been blinded by prevailing notions. We want to model for the world the delight of transcendent meaning in sexual union and open people's eyes to larger implications beyond their immediate decisions.

We who believe in a gracious Creator trust that our Designer's idea for our sexuality is a good one. We believe that if we follow God's instructions for our sexuality, we will be most fulfilled. (When I talk with kids about their sexuality it is not because I want to "spoil their fun" with old-fashioned restrictions, but because I want to invite them to the most satisfying sexual life possible. I think our society is giving them a rotten story. The Bible has a much better idea for how to live and how to be sexually fulfilled.)

1. Philosopher Peter Kreeft describes "Modernity's Loss of Faith in Ultimate Meaning" as the second of seven reasons why "Modernity Can't Understand Suffering." See chapter 10 of Kreeft's *Making Sense Out of Suffering* (Ann Arbor: Servant Books, 1986), pp. 167-84.

Only as Christians do we have the freedom of knowing that we are forgiven for our sexual sins. Jesus says that any of us who looks lustfully at another person commits adultery, so probably all of us are guilty. We all have regrets about our own confusions between social and genital sexuality, about our frantic attempts to get affection, or about our mistaken sexual choices. But we are forgiven, and we can begin again to make better choices. (When I talk with kids about "sex," I know that some in the room have already engaged in genital experimentation. I want to assure them of forgiveness and invite them to begin afresh by the grace of God to choose sexual faithfulness.)

Only as Christians do we know with delight that the Holy Spirit will empower us to be faithful in our deliberate sexual choices. It is difficult for Christians to choose to follow the instructions of the Designer when our milieu is saturated with suggestive displays and ridicules us for our biblical sexual perspectives. Yet we choose gladly, for the Spirit indwells us and floods us with satisfaction in our integrity. (When I talk with kids about "sex," I dare them to take God seriously and discover the great power available from the Holy Spirit for living intentionally the Christian alternative.)

The Bible Has a Better Idea

In her March 26, 1991, column, Ann Landers responded to a letter signed "Matter Over Mind in Massachusetts." The young man wrote that he was not able to get rid of bedroom thoughts about his girlfriend's other sexual partners when he saw them at social events or when he and "Molly" became intimate. He asked how to get rid of those thoughts because they were ruining their relationship.

That anguished man's letter made me profoundly sad, for it shows clearly one of the great tragedies of our times —

that in our culture's rejection of the "old-fashioned" ideas of biblical morality we have failed to see that God's design for human sexuality is a good one and that we reject it to our own peril. Sexual intercourse is such a profound sharing of ourselves with our partner that it needs to be protected — within the covenant of a lifelong, faithful commitment. When God's design is followed, how freeing it is for all the persons involved! For example, in his sexual relationship with me my husband knows that he never has to worry about past partners. Two of the men whom I had previously dated came to our wedding, and both continue to be friends with both my husband and me. Furthermore, my spouse can be totally confident that, as I was faithful to him *before* marriage, so I will be faithful *within* the marriage.

We who are God's people have a wonderful alternative to offer to the world around us. We encourage others to choose God's design for their sexuality — not to *spoil* their fun, but to *deepen* it; not primarily because they should fear AIDS and other sexually transmitted diseases, but because the psychological, social, and spiritual dis-ease from sexual unions outside of covenant protection in marriage is much more damaging. It is a great tragedy that the beauty of lifelong fidelity, the freedom of sexual purity, and the delight of sexual discovery with one and only one partner are never displayed and promoted by our society's advice columns.

4 The Church Must Be the Church: An Ethics of Character

The Christian Community Is an Alternative Society

The New Revised Standard Version finally translates this verse rightly: "If anyone is in Christ, *there is* a new creation" (2 Cor. 5:17, emphasis added). The reason why the Christian community is an alternative society is not that we are better than everybody else — more holy or wealthy or wise. We are able to offer alternatives to the world around us because our primary social location is not the technological milieu. We have been liberated from its values, its oppressions, its non-intimacy, and we have been brought by Christ into a whole new creation — namely, the reign of God. We don't have better ideas than our society about our sexuality, but God does, and we have the privilege (and the responsibility) to be God's ambassadors, proclaiming God's Kingdom principles and serving as agents of God's interventions in our world.

My emphasis on the Christian community as an alternative society does not promote a "we-they" mentality. Though we are ethically committed, we must watch carefully lest we become moralistic or have an attitude of superiority. Rather, this emphasis calls for a humble recognition that we cannot live very well on our own but desperately need the salvation of Christ and the empowerment of the Holy Spirit to find a way to live truthfully, in congruence with the Creator's design. Because of God's rich mercy toward us, we are enabled to respond by offering ourselves fully into doing gladly God's good and perfect will for human beings. Constantly we must keep watching lest we become more conformed to the values and behaviors of the technological milieu that surrounds us. Instead, enfolded in a community of caring people who support us and rebuke us and challenge us, we desire to be continuously transformed by the Holy Spirit's renewal of our minds (Rom. 12:1-2).[1] Then, gratefully and eagerly, we invite others to join us in the miracle of new life in union with Christ.

As an alternative society, the Christian community nurtures its children differently.[2] All of us in the community are responsible for helping youth to see that the values we hold as God's people provide for much better choices for how we live. We encourage our children to delight in nonconformity, to rejoice in the Spirit's transforming work in our lives. Thus, the sex education of our children begins when they are very tiny, for we want them from the very start to recognize the goodness of God's design, the truth of God's instructions, and the Joy of following them — not

1. See my comments on these verses and the emphasis on response to God's grace in the contrast of conforming/transforming in chapters 1–5 of *The Hilarity of Community* (Grand Rapids: William B. Eerdmans, 1992).

2. For a provocative study of what it means for the Church to form the character of its members both in and out of educational institutions, see the essays in *Schooling Christians*, ed. Stanley Hauerwas and John H. Westerhoff (Grand Rapids: William B. Eerdmans, 1992).

as duty, but as glad response to God's gracious revelation and invitation.

The world is desperate for better models. A few years ago I was invited to address seven "Family Living" classes at a public high school in Omaha. After I had presented the basic design of God (without using any religious terminology), the first question asked in each class was, "How do you *know* your husband is going to be faithful?" In this and the students' many other questions could be heard a great yearning for stability, for the assurance that relationships really could be permanent, for deep bonds. The next day I received thank-you notes from the kids, and they resoundingly affirmed what I had said and reported that they had passed it on to their boyfriends and girlfriends, their parents — even to a mother's boyfriend! One of the black leaders among the seniors insisted that the whole high school needed to hear this presentation and promised to work on making an assembly possible. These students liked the idea — the old-fashioned, biblical idea — that marriage could be permanent, that sexual union could be a special sign of a unique relationship. I had been saying for years that the world around us really wants what we as God's people know about sexuality. This experience and many others similar to it confirmed my belief. The Church has a great gift to offer our society, and many in our world long to hear it.

The Church's Failure in Sexual Matters

Why isn't the Church telling the world about God's design for sexuality? Why aren't we even telling our own members?

I first became involved in talking with kids about their sexuality at a summer camp for high school students. I agreed to do the presentation because it was to be held at the same time as water-skiing, so I didn't think many of the kids would show up. But they all did! And even though I did a terrible job of trying to tell them about the beauty of God's design, a surprising number of the youth came to thank me and insisted that they had never heard these ideas before — not from their parents or pastors or youth directors or Sunday school teachers. Though they live in a world that is constantly bombarding them with a false picture of sexual satisfaction, we who know better are failing to tell them that God has a better idea.

In this age when teenagers are looking for more stable sexual values, why isn't the Church offering strong guidance for friendships, protected sexual expression, and marriage? An editorial in *The Christian Century* reported the following response to the Presbyterian Church (U.S.A.) task force's 1991 report, "Keeping Body and Soul Together," which specifically endorsed sexual intercourse for unmarried persons and homosexuals:

> [Y]outh workers and youth themselves asked the church to provide clear moral boundaries. Holly Cammerer, a college student in Cincinnati, described her effort to resist the sexual permissiveness that prevailed on her campus and said: "I am disgusted that people like myself can no longer rely on the Presbyterian Church to support us in our moral stand." It was rather ironic, in view of the task force's avowed intent to listen to the sexually marginalized, that this woman felt marginalized for her embrace of traditional morality.[3]

One of the most telling indictments of the various church bodies' failure to provide clear, biblical moral guidance came from Camille Paglia, professor of humani-

3. David Heim, "Sexual Congress: The Presbyterian Debate," *The Christian Century* 108, 21 (26 June–3 July 1991): 643.

ties at the University of the Arts in Philadelphia, who in an article in *The New Republic* criticized the Presbyterian task force report (which was resoundingly rejected by the PCUSA General Assembly by a vote of 534 to 31!). She blasted the document for its "banal" language, its "simplistic" ideas, its "naive and sentimental" view of human nature, the "chaos and intellectual ineptitude" of its "fashionable liberal discourse," and its "contemporary platitudes and ignorance of world history and culture."[4] Though she does not use the word, what Paglia ultimately hates the most about the report is that it sought merely to move the line on *sin*, which she understands well, saying that "Eros . . . is a great and dangerous god" and that "Stormy nature, in our hearts and beyond the gates, is ready to consume us all." She summarizes the trend-following nature and shallowness of the report by declaring, "This is the kind of nonsense you get when you spend more time reading fifth-rate contemporary women writers than you do dead white males like Aeschylus and Shakespeare" (25). (We would add the Bible!)

Paglia wants Presbyterians to be true to their heritage and complains,

> In its laudable desire to remove the stigma from homosexuality, this document follows a strategy of distorting history. The Seventh Commandment forbidding adultery is never mentioned, while the overwhelming evidence that the Bible condemns homosexuality is blandly argued away piece by piece. This technique of disinformation has got to stop. Rational claims for social justice, as well as the critical search for a modern gay identity, cannot rest on lies. We must accept history for what it is, neither

4. Paglia, "The Joy of Presbyterian Sex," *The New Republic* 205, 23 (2 Dec. 1991): 24. Subsequent citations from this article will be given parenthetically in the text.

lightening nor darkening it to fit a ready-made political agenda. . . . Let us hear the worst that can be said, then define and know ourselves in relation to it. (26)

Understanding clearly that what churches are doing is muddying the clear biblical guidelines which make it possible to identify one's own rebellion, Paglia reproaches the Presbyterian committee for the document's "optimistic patter about 'empowerment' and 'mutuality' and its bliss-ful obliviousness to human perversity." She wants truth-fulness about human rebellion (27).

David Heddendorf summarizes her strongest attack as follows:

> Paglia surveys the committee's retreat from traditional Christian morality, sees a resultant lack of coherence and of checks against terrifying nature, and asks, "Why re-main Christian at all?" . . . [I]t's a tough-minded question, asking that a difference make a difference. . . . [F]or the pagan Paglia it isn't a rhetorical question. . . . She demands that we own up to a tough-minded Christian-ity — a Christianity that admits the rules and holds its ground — or else choose a paganism that acknowledges those rules just as frankly, then consciously breaks them. Heed the limits or find new ones; don't just explain them away.[5]

Paglia's critique is in my mind throughout this book as we seek to explore what difference it really does make to be a Christian, as we acknowledge human perversity and rebel-lion, even as we rejoice in God's forgiveness and the genuine "empowerment" of the Holy Spirit.

On a related concern, Marie Fortune, who has invested

5. Heddendorf, "A Pagan Protests Presbyterian Sex," *The Chris-tian Century* 109, 7 (26 Feb. 1992): 214.

much of her career in helping the Church face the issue of clergy sexual abuse of parishioners, bemoans the fact that church leaders do not take a strong stand to fight the problem. She commends Admiral Frank B. Kelso II for his unprecedented decisive action against naval officers in the scandalous "Tailhook" harassment case of 1992 and urges church bishops and presidents to do likewise. She suggests that the church leader

> could hold a press conference to announce the implementation of a comprehensive program of training and discipline designed to eradicate sexual abuse by clergy in his denomination. He could cite as motivation the disclosure of a research study that suggests that as many as 38 percent of clergy are sexually involved with their congregants. . . .
>
> The church leader could say [in imitation of the naval admiral], "The problem of sexual abuse by our clergy must stop. . . . Our congregations must be places of sanctuary where parishioners can assume that they will not be harmed or exploited. Our credibility as a church is on the line, and I will do everything in my power to remove those clergy who are responsible for the abuse. . . ."[6]

One assistant to a bishop of a mainline church body's regional office is primarily assigned to deal with sexual misconduct among clergy. It is a tragedy that such a staff position is necessary. To be the Church, we must do a better job of preventive medicine, of developing the Church as a community that nurtures its people to hold God's values for our sexuality.

Similarly, why have we allowed divorce to become so common in churches in direct contradiction of the biblical

6. Fortune, "How the Church Should Imitate the Navy," *The Christian Century* 109, 25 (26 Aug.–2 Sept. 1992): 765.

injunctions (Mal. 2:13-16; Matt. 5:31-32; 19:3-12)? Certainly the Church must learn better to bring healing love to those who are broken by the ravages of divorce, but we also could more thoroughly offer preventive medicine, urging the young to take seriously the permanence of marriage before they enter into it, exhorting those struggling with marital problems not to give up so easily, and standing by them with assistance for their practical needs. Those who want to keep trying in the face of a trying marriage need the support of the community to enable them to resist the pressure to conform to our society's pattern of easy divorce. Indeed, God's love is sufficient for the needs of those who must endure severe heartbreak and turmoil, but it needs to be incarnated in a caring community.

This book is a plea for the Church — its leaders and members — to develop and promote a comprehensive biblical ethic covering the entire range of sexual matters. The other sections of this book suggest possibilities for the major components of such an ethic. These are sketched along the lines of an "ethics of character," which is elucidated in the remainder of this chapter.

An Ethics of Character

Several aspects of an "ethics of character" will be noticeable in the suggestions of the rest of this book. If we outline these elements here, my sketches in the pages that follow will be more useful to you in forming sexual ethics for yourself and for the people you teach, counsel, or parent.

1. More Than Rules or Goals

An ethics of character has great advantages over the more traditional styles of ethics. An ethics of rules (deontology) in sexual matters often fails because of our natural human resistance to commands. If a parent lays down the law that her teenager is not to engage in sexual intercourse, the youth might rebel simply to provoke his parent. Though an ethics of character makes use of the same biblical commandments as part of the narratives which form our character, its focus is not on the rules themselves but on the kind of people we want to be. Moreover, the motivation lies, not in the rules as laws for behavior, but in the positive invitation of God's grace and in the delightful results of obedience.

The major disadvantage of an ethics of the end or of goals (teleology) is that too many factors in our life's experiences lie outside our control. Furthermore, we can rationalize all sorts of means toward an end because of the desirability of the goal. Many of us are aware of the more extreme examples of this type of guidance in the "situation ethics" of Joseph Fletcher. An ethics of character, in contrast, insists that the means must match the end, that we are concerned with who we are all along the way in pursuing any particular goal. Moreover, we are concerned about how each action in the process affects the development of our character.

2. Character Leads to Behavior

Deontological and teleological ethics are built primarily upon quandaries, real or imaginary. What should I do in a particular situation? What rule should I obey, or what goal will help me choose? Particular behavior is dictated by the issue of the moment.

In contrast, an ethics of character emphasizes that our particular behavior arises out of the kind of persons we are. My best illustration comes from a time when my husband and I were on the way to a doctor's office. We stopped at a red light, and when the light changed, the car in front of us did not move. Because it was a four-lane street, I kept turning around to look behind us and telling Myron that it was safe to go now. (Actually, nagging is what I was doing!) Finally, Myron leaned over to me and said gently, "I'm waiting to make sure the woman in front of us is all right."

I felt like a jerk. All I had been concerned about was getting to my appointment in time. Myron, being the considerate and thoughtful person that he is, was naturally concerned for the woman with car trouble.

I write *naturally* because it is in Myron's nature, his character, to be so observant of others' needs. Many factors contributed to the development of such a character — his parents' helpfulness to others, his own negative experiences as a small child picked on by bigger kids, his Christian beliefs. He IS a caring person, and consequently, when a situation arises, he will behave in a particularly caring way. (Now in the fourth year of our marriage, I keep hoping that the more I hang around with him the more his kind character will rub off on me! The models in our environment do form us!)

Our ethics of character for sexual matters, therefore, must ask what kind of people we want to be. The rules and goals of the Christian community are part of the narratives that help us to ask this question, but our emphasis will be on the *persons* who live out their sexuality in certain ways because of the kind of people they are.

add up to; accrue to

3. Behaviors Build Character

An ethics of character recognizes that life is a spiral. Certain behavior will arise out of a certain kind of character, and that behavior reinforces the character. If I want to be a kind person, I must be choosing kind acts that will develop habits and virtues.

I remember with shame one day many years ago in the

swimming pool when, out of frustration with another swimmer who kept bumping into me, I asked her, "Which lane are you swimming in anyway?" God would not let me go on that one, and as I swam to the opposite end of the pool my conscience tormented me. Perhaps it was not that poor woman's fault that she couldn't swim straight. (Now having lost most of my vision I know how difficult it can be.) I swam back as fast as possible to apologize to her, but she had left the pool. I raced into the locker room, but I could not find her. To this day that incident warns me to watch my tongue in the pool. I don't like the kind of rude person I was in that moment, and I don't want to develop such habits of thoughtlessness.

Each time a person chooses sexual faithfulness, that choice reinforces that kind of character. Each time someone allows himself to view pornographic materials, traits of exploitation are fostered. Whenever an individual uses sexually explicit language, she promotes vices of immodesty and hardens herself against the mystery and beauty of God's precious design for sexuality.

4. Nurturing Character

Church leaders, parents, teachers, youth directors, counselors — all of us who care about the sexual morality of the Christian community — must ask, then, what kinds of means we can use to develop certain traits of character in ourselves and in the youth of our congregations. Especially because we live in a milieu that bombards us with false notions about our sexuality, we must be very direct and careful to foster biblical perspectives.

We must ask precise questions about our milieu. Its comprehensiveness can be illustrated by comparing a fish, which must live in a milieu of water in order for its gills to draw out oxygen, with human beings, who must not be submerged in water in order to breathe. We thrive in

35

various milieus according to the kinds of people we are —
I enjoy an academic setting, while Myron flourishes in a
garden.

Moreover, all the factors of our environment affect our
development. If we eat a poisoned fish, we will become ill.
If a fish swims in toxic water, it will die. Many of the youth
in our society are growing up in a poisoned milieu of
violence, rage, and sexual exploitation. How can young
persons choose purity, celibacy, and faithfulness when they
are bombarded constantly by false values in sexually explicit movies, grossly overt genital language, suggestive
rock music, or pornographic magazines?

Those of us who care must take seriously the imperative need to create an alternative milieu. We dare not let
the moral indifference of our society immobilize us![7] Our
world desperately needs what the Christian community
has to teach about sexual character.

5. The Christian Community
as a Nurturer of Character

Long ago when I visited two convalescent centers weekly
to sing for the residents, I frequently noticed with delight
how easy it was to tell which persons had been spouses
for many years. After living together for a long time, they
had all of each other's mannerisms and phrases.

The apostle Paul observes the same phenomena in our
relationship with Christ. "But we all, with unveiled face,
beholding as in a mirror the glory of the Lord, are being
transformed into the same image from glory to glory, just
as from the Lord, the Spirit" (2 Cor. 3:18, NASV). The more
we behold Jesus, the more we will become like him as the
Holy Spirit transforms us into his likeness.

7. See S. Dennis Ford, *Sins of Omission: A Primer on Moral Indifference* (Minneapolis: Fortress Press, 1990).

The Christian community fosters that transformation in many ways. In the community's worship and Bible classes we hear and study the narratives that teach us who Jesus is and what his people are like. In the community's fellowship we experience the incarnation of those virtues. In the community's discipline we are rebuked and warned and instructed and loved when we choose values other than those of the Kingdom of God. In the community's strength we are bolstered with courage to continue holding fast to the truth about our sexuality in the face of the conflicting perspectives of the technological milieu. Because the Christian community is an alternative milieu, many facets contribute together to nurture godly character. But this will not happen automatically; it must be intentional and consistent and pervasive and strong and beautiful to provide an appealing alternative to our society's milieu.

6. The Narratives That Form Us

Because we are God's people, the Christian community will ask careful questions about the kind of sexual character we want to nurture. How does God's Word guide us as we seek the truth about our sexuality and God's design for its expression? What has been revealed by the biblical accounts of God's people in their sexual choices, in their instructions to each other? What virtues are displayed? What commands are issued that we ignore to our peril?

Especially the narratives of both Testaments are valuable because they expose the sexual idolatries that have endured throughout human history. The Scriptures also demonstrate the intertwining of other kinds of idolatry — greed, powermongering, covetousness — with sexual idolatry.

Moreover, the Bible gives us courage to deal with the sexual problems of our society because it announces to us the defeat of the principalities and powers. Those forces which contribute to the sexual pollution of our world have been defeated already by Christ (Col. 2:14-15), and we have been given the weapons of the Spirit to stand against all the methods of the demonic (Eph. 6:10-20). Truth is listed first as a primary component of our armor, and that is exactly what our culture needs. Our world is desperate for the truth about our sexual design and how the Creator intends for it to be maintained and enjoyed. There are many who will gladly choose God's intentions for their sexuality over the patterns of our society's behavior — if only we who know the truth will proclaim it more boldly!

7. An Ethics of Character Leads to Different Questions

The main task of ethics is to enable us to ask better questions about the issues of our day. An ethics of character is especially helpful because it gives us tools to ask new questions out of its comprehensive inclusion of means and ends, rules and narratives, models and virtues, personhood and community. Especially important is the fact that an ethics of character enables us to ask new questions out of the grace of God. We seek virtues and behaviors, not because we ought to, should, or must, but because they are modeled for us in Jesus, whose Spirit empowers us to follow in his way. We choose to live according to the design of the Creator because he invites us to the delights of such truthfulness. Moreover, we can invite others to participate in those choices, too, because we know that thereby they will be happier, more fulfilled, more whole.

This book is just a beginning. I pray that you will go beyond it to ask better questions about sexual character, to develop a Christian community that nurtures godly sexuality, to offer hope to those who are drowning in our society's toxic sexual milieu.

II God's Design for Sexual Character

When God made light, the angels
drew near to let the refractions roll
over their faces like a symphony.

When God made earth, they poked
their fingers into its moistness;
they put a fleck to their nose and smiled.

When God made the sea, they kicked
at the foam and sat in its cool
till their bones laughed.

When God made a rose, they parted
its petals and passed it among
themselves, saying, "So fragile,
yet how it grasps the soul."

When God made a giraffe,
they touched the strange hide
and murmured to themselves that God
was up to something magnificent.

SEXUAL CHARACTER

When God made man, each one
retired to his chamber and peered
into the writings, looking for some
clue to the mystery.

When God made woman, they came
back out of their chambers and gazed,
their jaws slack with awe.

When God joined man to woman
and said, "Let them become one flesh,"
everything suddenly made sense.
The cheering still shakes
the galaxies.

MARK LITTLETON

5 *Marriage Is for More Than Two*

In the previous section of this book we considered the importance of the Christian community being an alternative society. I grew up in an environment with such a spirit because my father was a Lutheran school principal, my mother was the school secretary, and both of them taught in the school. In addition, Mother was very active in literary and women's groups, and Father was the congregation's organist and choir director. We three children used to kid that we didn't grow up in a home, but in a school and church. I did not realize until graduate school how valuable that was, though at the time I knew intuitively that it was very special. I thought other children were deprived because they didn't get to stamp textbooks or move desks in the summer.

There were MANY advantages to growing up in such a home. We always knew the Christmas choir music especially well because we had heard our father composing it during the weeks of Advent. There never was any question about whether to tithe — that was the habit, firmly ingrained in all of us. There never was any question about whether to go to worship on Sunday mornings either. That day was special, and we prepared for it well.[1]

The greatest advantage was that we all knew, because of the involvement of our parents, that our family existed for more than ourselves. The question we asked about everything was whether it would enable us to serve God better. Would this purchase — or this use of our time, or this particular choice — contribute to the Kingdom of God?

My own personal decision came at age three. I resolved to be like my parents and serve God by teaching and making music. There was no better way to live; nothing could be more fulfilling.

I'm not referring to a decision for salvation; that is totally a gift of grace. This illustration points instead to decisions about life-style. For what does a family exist? Why is marriage valuable? These questions are especially important in these times when many reject marriage and simply live with someone for a while and when so many enter into marriage only until it no longer "works."

The biblical picture of marriage is certainly an alternative to the myths held by our society. In contrast to the romantic notions or the cynical ones, the Scriptures hold marriage in the highest esteem especially as a symbol of our relationship with God.

According to Genesis 1:28, one of the purposes for "male and female" is so that humankind can "be fruitful and multiply." However, the more precise picture in Genesis 2 of God's design for human marriage shows us something even more important than begetting children. In Genesis 2 God *fashions* a woman because the man is alone, on a different level from the animals and from God. (The Hebrew verb is the same one used when Solomon brings precious stones, costly jewels, and the choicest wood to

1. See my book *Keeping the Sabbath Wholly: Ceasing, Resting, Embracing, Feasting* (Grand Rapids: William B. Eerdmans, 1989).

42

fashion the Temple.) The LORD God forms her to be a "helper corresponding" to the man. This is an extremely powerful phrase for the biblical portrait of marriage because the noun *ezer* (helper) is most often used in the First Testament[2] for God. But God is a Helper infinitely superior to humankind. For true companionship and intimacy, the man needed a helper that corresponded to him. Indeed, for the woman to be named after God in this initial scene indicates right from the beginning of the canon that spouses represent God for each other on the human level in "corresponding" ways that can be understood. Marriage is designed for God's purposes, to imitate intimacy with God. Marriage exists for more than two.

That foundational hint is explicated thoroughly in Ephesians 5:21-33. Because that text has primarily been falsely used by churches to subjugate women, folks at conferences are always surprised when we go through the passage and chart its major subject. If we put marks in columns for Christ, the Church, the husband, and the wife whenever those subjects appear in the text, we discover that the primary subject of the text is not marriage but the relationship of Christ and his Bride! In fact, verse 32 explicitly says that the author is speaking of the profound mystery of Christ and the Church. The main purpose of marriage is to symbolize that, to display for all the world to see the mystery of Christ's fidelity to, and saving work for, his Bride.

Moreover, it corrupts the passage tragically to see in it a domination of men over women. When we consider what was going on in the society of Asia Minor at the time when this letter to the Ephesians was written, we will see clearly

2. I prefer to call the first three-fourths of the Bible the "First Testament" or the "Hebrew Scriptures," to avoid our culture's negative connotations of the name *Old* Testament and to emphasize the continuity of the biblical covenants with Israel and with Christians and the consistency of God's grace for his people.

that the passage calls for a dramatic alternative to the culture around the Christian community. Marriage served a political purpose, to witness to the world about the way in which everything is different when we belong to Christ and, in union with him, are ushered into a different milieu, the present reign of God.

When we analyze the structure of Ephesians 5 and 6, it is strikingly clear that the final verses of chapter 5 could not be picturing marriage, as some Christians claim, as a hierarchical chain of command — with God over the man, who chisels the wife (who pounds on the children, who beat on the dog!). Rather, the end of chapter 5 is part of a much larger whole, set between two passages about how to deal with the evil milieu that surrounds us. If we are going to walk as children of light (the emphasis which begins chapter 5), then we will want to be wise, to make the most of the time, to live by the power of the Spirit rather than by intoxication, to stand constantly on guard because the days are evil (5:15-20). Finally, we will recognize that the Christian life is thoroughly characterized by the battle against the principalities and powers, the "methods" of the demonic (6:10-20).

One particularly important way in which the Christian community "stands against" these forces of evil is outlined in 5:21–6:9. *Mutual submission* is the radical idea of the reign of God, which stands as a bright alternative to the dominations and subjugations of the world. The author of Ephesians gives three paired examples to show how mutual submission in the Christian community can counteract the functioning of principalities and powers in their milieu.

The first of these pairs, that of husbands and wives, is the one that concerns us in this chapter. We will look at the second pair, that of children and parents (6:1-4), in a later chapter (see Chapter 12, "Nurturing Children"). The third paired example, that of masters and slaves, offered a radical alternative to Ephesian society, for Christian masters were

44

encouraged to treat even slaves as fellow citizens of the household of God, and Christian slaves were urged to serve their masters as simply part of their willing service to the Lord.

The instructions to married couples are even more radical. In the Greek/Roman milieu of Asia Minor, men typically loved (with *erōs,* "passionate eroticism") their high-class prostitutes, cared for (with *storgē* or "family love") their wives, and most highly esteemed (with *philia,* the bonds of common interest) their friends. In great contrast, men in the Christian community were commanded to love their wives with an intelligent, purposeful love, directed toward the wives' needs *(agapē).* Moreover, this love was to be a symbol for all the world to see of Christ's love for his Bride, the Church. Their love for their wives was to illustrate the profound love that led Christ to submit to death in order to purify the Church.

Also, in great contrast to the surrounding society, in which wives were often not loved and were usually kept uneducated and in the house in order to raise fitting heirs for the husband's position, women in the early Christian community were enormously liberated. They were set free, first by Jesus himself, to be full participants in the community. Paul gives the trumpet call in Galatians when he insists that the community should be cut loose from all class, race, and gender barriers — that in the Body of Christ it makes no difference if you are slave or free, Jew or Gentile, male or female (3:28).

Unfortunately, it seems that some of the women got carried away with this new freedom, and consequently some corrective instructions had to be given by the apostle Paul. For example, in 1 Corinthians 11, he had to remind the women that when they led in worship by praying or prophesying they should be careful not to dress like prostitutes. They certainly were free, but to reject wearing the veil that characterized them as chaste women would be to cause offense, to tarnish the reputation of the Christian community. Similarly, they should not chatter in worship services or call across the aisle in the midst of things to ask their husbands questions. Since they had a lot of catching up to do, having been without much education, they could ask their husbands at home, but not in the middle of worship (1 Cor. 14:34-35).

So, too, in Ephesians 5, the women are encouraged not to let themselves get overly carried away by their new freedom in Christ. They were still to submit to their husbands as part of the mutual submission of the Church. This submission is no greater than that of their husbands — a point that is underscored by the construction of the text, for in 5:22 there is no verb and the whole phrase hinges on the mutual submission of verse 21. Furthermore, in verse 21 the verb is only a participle, one of a sequence of participles *(speaking, singing, making melody, giving thanks, submitting)* that show ways in which we live out the command (the imperative verb on which the participles depend) to be filled with the Spirit (v. 18). What radical activities — singing, praising, submitting! (Last night at rehearsal I told the choir members that they were engaging in the most radical activity by singing. In a world of political and economic chaos, we declare the sovereign reign of God. Our singing does not express what we feel or mean, but we sing truthful words that teach us to mean what they say!)[3]

Ephesians 5:21-33 thus shows an extremely careful dialectical balance. On the one hand, members of the community are set free in Christ to be equal. On the other hand, members are to submit to each other for the larger purpose of the witness of the community to the world. (The dialectic

3. See Marc Kolden, "Rollicking Advice for Evil Days: A Biblical Rationale for Christian Singing," *Word and World* 12, 3 (Summer 1992): 238.

is captured by Luther's paradoxical phrase, "The Christian is lord of everything and servant to none and servant of all and master of nothing.") In particular, husbands will not only submit to their wives but also will go far beyond that to love them with the very love of Christ for his Church. Women, out of their love for their husbands (which does not even need to be commanded), will recognize that their new freedom in Christ does not negate the call to mutual submission.[4]

Moreover, as we have previously seen, Genesis 1 invites God's people to live in relationship with each other in the mutuality of imaging God, with each person contributing his or her particular gifts, which reveal facets of God's grace. That picture, together with many other passages in the Scriptures that challenge us to use our gifts for the upbuilding of the Christian community (see, e.g., Rom. 12; 1 Cor. 12; Eph. 4; and 1 Pet. 4:10-11), enables us to place the marriage relationship and its contributions within the framework of the entire purpose of the Christian community.

For example, one of my goals in our marriage is to be as supportive as possible of Myron's elementary school teaching because that is one very important way in which he brings the reign of God to our world. Through his gentle care, especially for the children from troubled homes, he enfolds them in the different reality of the love of God. But to care persistently for dysfunctional children is extremely wearing, and so my tasks must include practical ways to uplift him and give him rest and encouragement.

Similarly, Myron's understanding of our marriage includes his support of my teaching and writing. Often he

---

4. A thorough explication of this text can be found on my teaching tape #330, " 'Wives, Submit!': A New Look at Ephesians 5," available from Dottie Davis, CEM Tape Ministry Coordinator, 15500 N.E. Caples Road, Brush Prairie, WA 98606.

takes on extra household chores so that I can work on the speaking engagements or writing projects that we believe I am called to do.

We know that the Scriptures challenge us to direct our marriage outside of itself. Its primary purpose is not merely to satisfy ourselves and rest comfortably in each other's love. Rather, its major purpose is to be an agent of the Kingdom of God, to bring God's reign to bear on the world around us. In most marriages, that happens not only through outside involvements, but especially through bearing children and passing on to them the heritage of the faith. Since my handicaps prevent us from having children, Myron and I can invest instead in others' children in our teaching and writing.

Out of a similar biblical perspective, Stanley Hauerwas calls marriage a "heroic institution."[5] He emphasizes that marriage

> stands as one of the central institutions of the political reality of the church, for it is a sign of our faithfulness to God's Kingdom come through the providential ordering of history. . . . Our commitment to exclusive relations witnesses to God's pledge to his people, Israel and the church, that through his exclusive commitment to them, all people will be brought into his Kingdom.
>
> Marriage so understood is a heroic task that can be accomplished only by people who have developed the virtues and character necessary for such a task. The development of such virtues and character is a correlative of a narrative that helps us understand that struggle in which we are involved. But it is exactly such a narrative

5. See Hauerwas, "The Public Character of Sex: Marriage as a Heroic Institution," in his book *A Community of Character: Toward a Constructive Christian Social Ethic* (Notre Dame: University of Notre Dame Press, 1981), pp. 184-93.

that we have been lacking, or perhaps more accurately, our primary problem is that our experience of marriage has been captured by narratives that have done little for, and have perhaps even perverted, the role of marriage in the Christian community.[6]

Our culture's primary myth of romantic love is certainly inadequate as a foundational understanding for Christian marriage. We see its effects in the disturbingly high divorce rate in our society, for in many persons' minds when the romance fails the marriage is over.

Most of the people who talk with me about marriage sketch its major focus in how they care for each other. Such a perspective causes the marriage to be, in Martin Luther's phrase, "inward turned," and such a convolution is difficult to sustain. Marriage needs a larger focus, a greater goal outside itself. An infinite goal (to live according to the purposes of God) is truly fulfilling — because it cannot be reached, but integrates the whole of a person and the couple in the constant desire for faithfulness. In contrast, a finite goal, even if it is reached, can never satisfy because it only integrates one aspect of life. My parents' marriage had enormous strength through times of stress and scant financial resources because their lives were directed beyond themselves to serving God in the congregational music program and school.

Lest we think that all the discussion of this chapter turns marriage into an onerous burden of duty and Christian responsibility for the bearing of God's Kingdom, we must not forget that the Scriptures also contain the Song of Solomon. Other poems in the Bible also parallel the Song's exuberant celebration of love and passionate desire and devotion.

Again, the biblical picture offers an important dialectic

6. Hauerwas, *A Community of Character*, p. 191.

that must be kept in balance. God's design for our sexuality certainly includes desire and sexual fulfillment, but these factors are not supreme. To recognize larger purposes in marriage enables us to avoid the sexual idolatries that characterize our culture. We remember that God alone is to be worshiped. Our lives together in marriage empower us more thoroughly in that worship — not only because we support each other's involvements in the work of the Kingdom, but also because our very sexual celebration is also an experience of worship and gratitude to a Creator who designed such a beautiful expression of our intimate bond in marriage.

These dialectical balances — of sexual celebration without idolatry and of mutual submission and *agapē* love — and their larger context change the nature of our commitment to each other in marriage. Now all the kinds of love named by the four Greek words mentioned earlier (purposeful love directed to the needs of the other, and the loves of friendship, family ties, and eroticism) are intertwined together within our commitment to the purposes of God. Such an understanding of marriage requires the support of the entire Christian community. As Stanley Hauerwas emphasizes,

> A true "realism" requires a community that forms our loyalties in such a manner that both the costs and hopes of marriage can be properly held in balance. Only from such a perspective can we reach a more profound sense of the relation of love and marriage, as it is only within such a context that we can begin to understand that the love properly characteristic of marriage is not a correlative of the attractive qualities of our mates. Only a love so formed has the capacity to allow the other freedom to be other without resentment.[7]

7. Hauerwas, *A Community of Character*, p. 194.

In addition to the importance of a community that supports us in this kind of commitment and that forms and nurtures such a love, the Body of the Church could also be much more helpful than it customarily is to those who are contemplating marriage. I learned while participating in a Mennonite community the value of "calling a meeting to discern the Spirit." Consequently, when my dear friend of seven years proposed, we decided to spend two weeks gathering the input of the Christian community before we made a final decision. What a wonderful process that was! We asked many people — single and married, those who might be opposed to the idea, even someone who was also dating me who had jokingly insisted that if Myron ever proposed he wanted to have a chance to make a counterproposal! How helpful it was to us — as we contemplated such issues as my many physical handicaps, our differences in education, our age, and our diversities of interests — to know that our friends and colleagues in the Church were praying with us and for us. We asked them to give us specific advice and to ask us questions that would help us to think more clearly.

A decisive turning point for me came when one of my best friends widened my perspectives. She asked me what my primary criterion was for making the decision. I answered that the most important question was, "Will marriage to Myron help me serve God better?" But that question usually resulted in what seemed a tie — I could serve God better if I were free to travel to teach anywhere at any time, or I could serve God more effectively if I were more deeply rooted in a home. Marguerite proposed that I should ask instead if marriage to Myron would enable me to *love* God better. That made an enormous difference and brought my questioning more thoroughly in line with the biblical picture of marriage as a symbol of God's faithfulness. There was no doubt about it: Myron's gentle care would certainly enfold me in, and constantly remind me

51

of, God's grace and love, and consequently would set me more free to respond in love to God.

It is for the purposes of the community of God's people that marriage is so important — for nurturing children to carry on the faith, for reaching out to the world with the alternatives of the reign of God. The community, therefore, must provide the narrative in which we can understand marriage in the framework of these larger goals of loving and serving God.

6 *Sexual Union Is More Than "Sex"*

One of the main aspects of its narrative that the Christian community must proclaim to our world is the biblical understanding of sexual union. The Scriptures provide perspectives, instructions, illustrations, and rebukes to form our character and instill the necessary virtues.

The biblical perspective is strategically introduced right at the beginning of the canon. Genesis 1:28 records God's command for the fruitfulness of human union — a topic usually removed entirely from discussions of sexuality. Because the subject of children is so important a consideration in sexual matters, we will reserve it for more thorough discussion in Chapters 12 and 13 and focus here on the act of sexual intercourse itself.

The initial account of Genesis 2:18-24 significantly commands the man to *leave* his father and mother and *cleave* to his wife. Those two verbs are strong; they denote a decisive change of orientation, a movement away from one's family of origin and a profound commitment and faithfulness to, and bonding with, one's spouse.[1] Only then do the man

1. In the midst of the patriarchy of Semitic cultures, this is an

and woman become "one flesh." This name for sexual union is especially important, for it indicates this profound mystery in God's design for human sexuality: sexual union creates a uniquely comprehensive bond. To tear it apart fractures every dimension of an individual's whole being. To stitch that bond with more than one partner causes a schizophrenic *psyche* (the Greek word for "soul").

Remember the typewriter: its designers created it in such a way that the typing and correcting ribbons can function together without interfering with each other. To ignore the designers' instructions for threading and maintaining the ribbons is to jam the works.

The loving Creator of our human sexuality instructed us to celebrate sexual union only with our spouse. He graciously warned us of the dangers and the consequences of fornication and adultery, of promiscuity and betrayal. To ignore the Designer's instructions is to rupture our spirits and souls, to destroy the possibility for that union to carry the significance and delight for which it was intended.

After many years of counseling and observing, I write this with great anguish. How I long for young people in our society to enjoy the exquisite gift of sexual intercourse as a special sign of covenant promising, of permanent commitment to one and only one person! So many kids never have the chance to learn of that precious possibility. If they are constantly bombarded by the violence of our society's raw sex and flagrant promiscuity, can they ever appreciate the gentle fragrance of this sweet rose, the holy purity of

---

astounding statement. First of all, the man is the one commanded, and second, he is instructed to be faithful to one spouse. In contradiction of a common assumption that the Bible also is patriarchal, I want to urge its readers to recognize that, from the very beginning of the canon and throughout both Testaments, the Bible offers an alternative to the world around it and calls for gender and race egalitarianism and mutuality in relationships.

a genuinely chaste union, rich with sexual pleasure and delight?

I think that our vocabulary both creates and reflects our attitudes. The common slang expression "to make love" does not accurately describe what happens in the sexual union of committed marriage partners. Love is *made* all the time in a marriage — when together we clean up the kitchen, sing a hymn side by side in a worship service, ride our bicycles to the neighborhood park, talk on the porch swing about the day's work, play a game, plan for the future, or remember the past. Love grows when, apart from each other, we speak lovingly about our spouse, work at our jobs with a sense of the other's support, or plan surprises. The way the phrase "to make love" is used in our society, it might rather show some of the emptiness of trying to invent love for a partner for whom there is not such a consistent investment in love-generating and with whom there is no protective framework of covenant promising.

Myron and I use instead the expression "to say love." Because we continue to learn many more ways to love each other (with all four kinds of love), we are so grateful to have this unique union to say it. Words are inadequate (even though we make up new ones and try all sorts of combinations) to express how deeply devoted we are to each other. How glad we are that God ordained such a special way to "say love," to tell each other in a way that we tell no one else in the whole world that we will be faithful to each other for all of our lives! Because there are so many other undergirding intimacies — spiritual, intellectual, aesthetic, social, financial, emotional, physical (as in shared sports), playful (as in hobbies and games) — we say love in many moods and with all kinds of nuances. Whether the love-saying is wild and passionate or gentle and consoling, whether it is laughing and crazy or serious and divulging, it always speaks faithfulness.

Each time that we say love it is a covenant, a spiritual act. It is a reminder that we have promised to be faithful, that we are knit together in this special bond of oneness for the purposes of God.

Our society thinks that the experience of sexual intercourse can become boring, ordinary, routine. Certainly that can be the case when sexual union only means the act itself, and its value is measured in decibels of excitement. To put all the weight of the experience on its level of physical stimulation is an unreasonable burden — and the pressure of that burden often decreases the feelings of pleasure and delight.

However, for those who are God's people, sexual union always means much more. Though the actual physical experience itself might not even be very wonderfully pleasant, yet the act of sexual union points beyond itself. It is the symbol of God's commitment to us, the sign of our covenant promising to our spouse, the expression of our permanent faithfulness. To say that is a great gift, the gift of truth, which does not depend upon how one feels about it. The lovely result is that the positive feelings are often multiplied because they can be the afterglow of all the meaning, instead of having to carry the weight of meaning by themselves.

My physical handicaps have made all of this more apparent to me. If the meaning of sexual intercourse lies only in the heightened stimulations of physical beauty or pleasure, then its meaning is totally lost when a person ages or becomes infirm. In fact, we see that often in our society when middle-aged men or women leave their spouses for younger, more attractive partners. My debilitations deepen my awareness of how little the momentary sensations of physical ecstasies matter. The greatest gift of sexual union is its truth — the assurance that this man is committed to me for life, the divine call that our marriage is to be a sign of God's grace, the security that love does not depend upon our attractiveness or sexual prowess.

There is enormous security in knowing that our

marriage isn't built on the single pillar of sexual pleasure. I don't have to worry all the time, as many in our society do, that my sexual partner might become disappointed or dissatisfied with our sexual life. A relationship built on the single pillar of sexual fulfillment is bound to tip over. Because the many supports of all kinds of intimacies hold up our marriage, the love-saying doesn't have to prove anything. It can simply tell the truth — and that alone is overwhelmingly beautiful.

Moreover, when sexual union has been reserved for one and only one relationship, its pleasure is not marred by any comparison of experiences with other partners. Remember the student's question, mentioned in Chapter 1, after my workshop at a Christian college on "When to Say 'Yes' to Sex." He asked, "What if you save sex for marriage, and then it isn't good?" Because I was single at the time, I responded from my head by asking what he meant by "good" and pointing out the goodness of promising and of commitment over against the fleeting goodness of a physical moment. Then a married professor at the school answered from the heart, "What is good about my sex life is that everything I know about it I have learned *with* my wife. We never have to wonder if our spouse is comparing our sexual skill with that of someone else. Instead, we discover together what gives us pleasure and what is good."

What makes sexual intercourse good is knowing that it is the special secret of the married lovers and that its meaning points beyond itself. How can a person who "makes love" with many partners have any unique way to "say love" in a trustworthy promising? How can anything be *said* in sexual union if the act has been emptied of its covenant meaning?

Besides its significance as a special statement of a unique and promised permanent relationship, sexual union must be understood within the wider framework of our human imaging of God. As we have emphasized

57

throughout this book, our sexual expression is just one of many ways in which the Christian community holds before the world an alternative life-style that reflects the values of the Kingdom of God.

Many times in the First Testament, especially in the story of the prophet Hosea, God illustrates by means of human sexuality his faithful covenant love for Israel and her infidelity. The sexual lives of God's people, therefore, are always judged by this question: Are we symbolizing God's fidelity or imitating Israel's faithlessness?

The question is critically important for those of us who deeply desire to be the agents of God's purposes in the world. Only with integrity of character can we invite the world to witness the faithfulness of God.

The intertwined relationship of sexuality and spirituality is emphasized throughout the Scriptures by the frequency with which God uses sexual images to admonish Israel. Rebukes for "going awhoring after other gods" occur almost twenty times in the First Testament, revealing the interconnection between making sexual intercourse an idol and giving our love promiscuously to any of a multiplicity of other gods.

The profound damage that is done to life and faith and the witness of the community when God's design for sexual union is violated is suggested by the severity of the punishment called for in Israel. Fornicators and adulterers were to be stoned. If one cannot live in a holy way, one should not live.

It is imperative in our reading of such severe passages that we do not put the cart before the horse. Such proscriptions in the Scriptures are not given so that God's people avoid adultery merely out of fear of punishment. Rather, the canonical construction (and God's grace!) invites us first to appreciate God's design, and only afterwards are we told about the consequences of failure. To emphasize only the law without the gospel undergirding it is to miss the intent of God's Word. Even the foundational commandments do not simply say "Thou shalt" and "Thou shalt not." Instead, they begin with the words, "I am the LORD your God, who brought you out of the land of Egypt" (Exod. 20:2, RSV). This is the God who created us, who saved us, who set us free from the Egyptian bondage, who led us out of captivity to other gods. Now here are the instructions for living fully his creative design, in response to his saving interventions on our behalf.

Furthermore, the Scriptures do not distinguish sexual sins as being any worse than other forms of rebellion against our Creator. Both fornicators and the greedy violate the values of the Kingdom of God. All sins are idolatrous; all come out of unbelief. All sins separate us from God; all mar the witness of the community. All sins are equally serious; all are equally forgiven. All sinners are enabled to change by the grace of God's forgiveness, the power of the Holy Spirit, and the support of the community.

The Scriptures also record many examples of persons violating God's ordinances for their sexuality. As the apostle Paul says, "These were written for our instruction" (1 Cor. 10:11, NASV). They stand as gracious warnings of the consequences, for God is interested in our well-being and wants to help us avoid the pain and fracturing that result when we choose to make "sex" our god.

This chapter has explored some of the tragedies caused by our society's understanding of genital sexual expression and some of the gifts of God's design for human sexuality. How can we in the Church help our young people to avoid the tragedies and at the same time to know the possibility of these gifts and to desire their treasure?

As Stanley Hauerwas bemoans, "Current reflection about sexual ethics by Christian ethicists is a mess."[2] In the

2. Hauerwas, *A Community of Character* (Notre Dame: University of Notre Dame Press, 1981), p. 175.

midst of the sexual anarchy of our culture, the Christian community should be the locus of clear thinking about the issues and clear proclamation of God's design. We can serve our youth best if the Church decisively affirms the biblical narratives, upholds the traditional values of sexual union (without the customary legalism or denunciation of delight), and models the beauty of covenant-promising faithfulness.

7 *The Virtues of Sexual Character for Marriage as a Heroic Enterprise*

Often when I am speaking to various groups about God's design for our sexuality (or almost any other topic!), someone suggests that I am speaking too naively, too idealistically, too optimistically. But those terms do not accurately name what I am doing, for they seem to imply that what I am describing is impossible or that my words are untrue or unreal.

However, if my words are simply making clear the biblical picture, then they are much more true and more real than those advocating the sexual promiscuity and inanity of our society. The Scriptures show us the real and tragic consequences of choosing sexual behaviors outside of God's design for human sexuality, and they offer a true and promising vision of what life can be like if it is lived faithfully.

How desperately our world needs the biblical visions! In our chaotic culture, many persons yearn for hope that their sexual lives could be more meaningful, that relationships could be permanent, that lasting happiness wouldn't constantly elude them.

The task of the Church, then, in sexual matters is to

proclaim the visions of God, to invite the world around us into the values of God's Kingdom, to model lives of faithfulness. What kind of persons should we be to support the mission of the Church?

As in all other aspects of life, to fulfill the purposes of God and to accomplish the mission of the Church in sexual matters, we need to be persons like Jesus. All the character traits exhibited by him in the Gospel accounts are virtues that we pray will be formed in ourselves. As the apostle Paul writes to the Philippians, we want to be persons who have the mind of Christ (2:5). Lest that be too overwhelming for us to think about, however, let us focus our attention on a representative sampling of the virtues of Jesus.

One of the best pictures of the virtues necessary to be persons able to live out the visions of God is given by Paul's listing in Galatians 5:22-23 of the fruit of the Spirit. We cannot live as God intended us to live without the empowerment of the Spirit at work in our characters.

It is necessary to note that in Galatians 5:22 both the noun *fruit* and the verb *is* are singular. There is only one fruit of the Spirit — the life of Christ formed in us — but it has many manifestations. I stress this to combat a common teaching in many Christian circles that a person must try to get more of a certain kind of fruit in his or her life.

This teaching falsely puts pressure on an individual to crank up a certain aspect of personality. In truth, we each have unique personalities that display various proportions of the different manifestations of the fruit of the Spirit. My personality is much more exuberant; my husband's is much more gentle. I don't need to struggle to manufacture more of the "peace fruit" in my life, nor does Myron need to crank up more "Joy fruit." God created the diversity of our personalities, and the Spirit makes use of precisely who we are. If we were all the same, we wouldn't be able to minister to the varieties of people there are in the world.

The more we allow the Spirit to work in us the more truly we will reflect the life of Christ and the more thoroughly our lives will express the fruit of the Spirit according to the God-created proportions of our unique personal beings.

This interpretation does not mean that we shouldn't desire to exhibit the fruit more thoroughly. Of course, we who are God's people want to be controlled more fully by the Spirit and not by our sinful natures. I am merely combating the false teaching that if someone doesn't have a peaceful personality then there is something wrong with his spiritual life. I have seen too many Christians not appreciate their own unique proportion of the nine manifestations of the Christ-life fruit because of this false teaching.

Moreover, there are myriads more manifestations of the fruit than these nine aspects. That this listing is symbolic is underscored by the fact that Paul lists nine. It can be easily observed that Paul uses symbolic numbers frequently, and the number three for Jewish people always means divine (even in the First Testament before they knew about the Trinity). To list three sets of three accentuates the message that, when the Spirit controls us, our lives will display "divinely divine" character and virtues.

"But the fruit of the Spirit is love, joy, peace, patience, kindness, goodness, faithfulness, gentleness, self-control" (Gal. 5:22-23, NASV). One skill that we worked on just yesterday in my Sunday morning Bible class is in noting the connecting words when we study the Bible.[1] The connector *But* in this verse reminds us again that the virtues of the Christian life are an alternative to the character of those who are outside the Kingdom of God.

Immediately before Paul's listing of the fruit of the Spirit, he had emphasized that God's people will not

1. For a discussion of the importance of the word *therefore* in Paul's writings, see chapter 1 of my book *The Hilarity of Community* (Grand Rapids: William B. Eerdmans, 1992).

manifest the deeds of the flesh, which include the following (note the three listed first!): "immorality, impurity, sensuality, idolatry [including sexual], sorcery, enmities, strife, jealousy, outbursts of anger, disputes, dissensions, factions, envyings, drunkenness, carousings, and things like these" (Gal. 5:19-21, NASV). You probably noticed that many of the other behaviors on this list often occur in conjunction with sexual immorality — such things as jealousy, enmities, carousings, or almost any of the other things that Paul mentions.

Verse 21 continues, "of which I forewarn you just as I have forewarned you that those who practice such things shall not inherit the kingdom of God" (NASV). To behave in such ways is to live outside the reign of God, to miss out on the gifts of the Kingdom. *But* there is an alternative. *But*, Paul says, there is the life empowered by the Spirit, the life modeled by Christ, the life designed by God, and it is manifested in various divine virtues, such as the nine that follow.

The construction of this section of Galatians reveals that the visions of God are not just naive idealism or false optimism. They offer the true hope that certain virtues, formed by the Spirit, can issue in behavior that is different from that manifested by those who are controlled by their own corrupted natures. The sexual idolatries, manipulations, and abuses of our world can be counteracted. But it requires the nurturing of godly virtues, the developing of personal integrity and character, manifesting a life that follows Jesus.

There is very little variation as different translations list the symbolic nine manifestations. The Church has quite consistently understood the picture that Paul gives of the virtues of the Christian life. We will be concerned especially about how these virtues will influence sexual behavior.

Love

Many youth have asked me, "But isn't it all right to have sex with my boyfriend if I really love him?" Their question demonstrates how tragic it is that the English language contains only one word *love* and that this word has become so inane. People use it to describe their craving for hamburgers, their adulations of rock stars, or their sentimental romantic notions, as well as their unharbored lusts.

Quite significantly for our purposes in this book, Paul lists *agapē* as the first Spirit-empowered virtue. In classical Greek, this kind of love was the least valued, for *agapē* meant a disinterested love. The ancient philosophers treasured much more highly a friendship love *(philia)*, which emphasized the cultivation of common interests. Some philosophers warned against the entanglements of erotic love *(erōs)*, and there seems to be a bit of condescension in their call for affectionate love for human beings *(philanthrōpia,* from which we get our common word for charity).

In contrast, the earliest Christians took over the word *agapē* to describe the inexplicable love of God, that he should love so fully, so freely, so wisely, without needing our love in return for his to continue. Consequently, as applied to the followers of Jesus, that word challenges us to imitate his love, with all of its focus on caring concern, thoughtful and purposeful action, and high regard for each human being. It is important to note that every New Testament command to love others utilizes the verb forms of *agapē*.[2]

2. Johannes P. Louw and Eugene A. Nida, eds., *Greek-English Lexicon of the New Testament Based on Semantic Domains* (New York: United Bible Societies, 1988), vol. 1, pp. 293-94, 25.43. References to Greek definitions in this book are taken from this lexicon because its approach and methodology make use of the insights of modern linguistics and its definitions are based upon the distinctive features of meaning of a particular term in comparison with, and in contrast to, other related words in the same semantic domain.

The intelligence and purposefulness implied in the name of this virtue makes it much easier to answer youths' questions about "having sex" if they "really love someone." We know that if indeed we genuinely love another with God's kind of love, we won't want to "jam the works" of that person's sexual wholeness by taking the act of sexual union out of its context of covenant promising and permanent faithfulness. To love others truly means to care more about the connection between their future well-being and present faithfulness than about our immediate sexual gratification.

Joy

To be persons of Joy also makes a great difference in our sexual behavior, for the Greek word *chara* designates a profound gladness not at all associated with circumstantial happiness or immediate gratification.[3] In a world where genital sexuality is integrally intertwined with attitudes demanding one's rights to pleasure, the Christian community offers the alternative of learning to appreciate the profound Joy of living within God's design and the more satisfying delight of long-term faithfulness rather than instant highs.

Many scramble after "sex" because they want to be happy. The Bible reminds us instead that Joy is a Spirit-given virtue, that when we direct our lives to fulfilling God's purposes in the world, then we will experience as a by-product the fullness of a Joy that is not limited by human circumstances.

If our lives are characterized by the Joy of being part

3. For a more thorough explication of the biblical word *Joy*, see chapter 12 of my book on the Psalms, *I'm Lonely, LORD — How Long?* (New York: Harper & Row, 1983). I always capitalize the word *Joy* in my writing to signify the qualities outlined here in contrast to merely human happiness.

of the Kingdom of God, then we will not "need" to satisfy our sexual desires in ways contrary to God's design. Joy empowers us to wait, to be patient, to choose carefully, to be faithful. As can be readily seen, each of the virtues on Paul's list reinforces and is strengthened by the others.

Joy is an essential ingredient in Christian marriage because it enables partners to keep their priorities rightly ordered. The point of Christian marriage is not to find our happiness in each other, but together to find great Joy in being God's servants. The gift of Joy binds us together even when our particular circumstances — financial, physical, or whatever — are not especially happy.

Similarly, Joy is also an especially valuable virtue in Christian singleness. Whereas the world around us hammers us with the cultural idea that our lives are not complete if we are not "having sex" with someone, I did not experience such a lack of wholeness in the years before I married Myron. The Spirit gave great Joy in my work as an itinerant Bible teacher, through deep friendships with many others in the Body of Christ, and from my own personal devotional life. It seems to me that Joy is a primary virtue both for whole contentment in singleness and celibacy and for enabling us to bring to a marriage relationship a wholeness that is not desperate for another person to "find happiness."

Peace

Because he was Jewish, when Paul chose the Greek word *eirēnē* for his symbolic list of virtues he probably had in mind the concepts of the Hebrew word *shalom*. For Jews the latter word conveys a great sense of wholeness, founded in peace with God and issuing in peace with others and with one's self. Such peace leads to health, wealth, fulfillment, satisfaction, contentment, well-being.

The tranquility and freedom from anxiety suggested by *shalom* arise from this truth: peace is an established fact, made possible by God's grace.

Because of its emphasis on wholeness, it is easy to see why peace is a very important virtue in a personal character that will beget godly sexual behavior. If an individual is at peace with God, then he will accept and gladly choose God's design for his sexuality. If a person knows wholeness and peace within herself, she will not feel desperate for someone else to "make her whole." Our peace with God, with others, and with ourselves will prevent us from sexually manipulating, coercing, abusing, or harassing others. If God's people know the satisfaction and contentment of a total commitment to God's purposes in the world, then that long-term fulfillment will hold in check the need for immediate gratification.

Of course I am writing about the ideal. I know the intense loneliness and despair that cause us at times to want to manipulate others to serve our sexual desires. That is why we need to recognize that peace is a corporate virtue. (All the other virtues on this list require community, too, but it is especially noticeable with peace because of how strongly the New Testament builds on the corporate nature of the Hebrew concept.) We cannot know God's *shalom* by ourselves. We need the Christian community to remind us, to enfold us in its reality, to nurture the virtue in us. As with all the virtues on this list, none of us knows perfect peace. But Paul holds before us a vision of what kind of people we can be if we let the Holy Spirit take over in our lives, and we see especially for our purposes here that to be that kind of a person is exactly what is needed to live out God's design for our sexuality.

In offering helps for those who translate the Bible into other languages, Johannes Louw and Eugene Nida suggest that the freedom from anxiety, inner turmoil, and worry that *eirēnē* conveys might be best captured by such ethnic idioms as "to sit down in the heart," "to rest in the liver," or "to be quiet in one's inner self."[4] These idioms describe well the kind of persons who are empowered to be obedient to God's alternative vision of sexuality.

Patience

Similarly, the ethnic idioms that Louw and Nida suggest for the Greek noun *makrothymia* or patience ("longsuffering" in the KJV) invite us to imagine a quality of character that will affect our sexual behavior in many ways. The virtue of patience enables one "to remain seated in one's heart," "to keep from jumping in one's heart," or "to have a waiting heart."[5]

Each of these expressions brings to mind another necessary aspect of sexual godliness. For example, the image of remaining seated graphically portrays the steadfastness and commitment of patience in sexual matters. I am always amazed and gratefully overwhelmed by Myron's continued commitment to me in spite of the proliferation of my physical problems since we have been married. He remains seated beside me, in great contrast to three of my friends' husbands, who left them when they became handicapped visually, physically, and emotionally. To remain sexually faithful to one's spouse in the face of misfortune requires a character strong in Spirit-given patience.

The image of not "jumping in one's heart" builds on the connotation in *makrothymia* that one maintains a state of emotional calm in the face of provocation. Many marriages end in conflicts or disputes that are not resolved because one or both parties cannot refrain from "jumping in the heart." We need an enormous amount of patience

4. Louw and Nida, *Greek-English Lexicon*, vol. 1, p. 315.
5. Louw and Nida, *Greek-English Lexicon*, vol. 1, p. 307.

with our spouses to continue living together in forgiveness rather than nurturing complaints or irritations that compound the problems. Many of the virtues in Paul's list enable a person to continue forgiving, a necessary ingredient in sexual faithfulness.

The last ethnic image, "to have a waiting heart," is especially important for the unmarried in our society. Because our culture keeps urging young people to take what they can get while they can, our world needs profoundly the Christian alternative model of being able to reject immediate sexual gratification as an act of desire. By Spirit-empowered patience, we choose instead to wait until the bond of "love-saying" is enfolded in, and expressive of, a permanent covenantal union.

Kindness

The Greek term *chrēstotēs* or kindness highlights the type of acts that proceed from this virtue. To have a character of kindness means that a person will behave in ways that provide something beneficial for others. This virtue is especially important for our purposes in this book because of the immense need in our society for the affirming, uplifting, and nurturing of persons.

How significant for helping single persons to remain celibate are the little deeds of kindness that help to support them in their choices, that hold up their trampolines of personal identity. How important are the inexpensive gifts of kindness that spouses offer each other to nurture their affection and promote their faithfulness. How valuable are the seemingly insignificant moments of kindness in the nurturing of children. All of these actions of kindness may seem small, and yet their possibilities for changing the world are enormous.

What difference might it make in a child's ability to

reserve his genital sexuality for marriage if his social sexuality is upheld each day by a loving note in his lunchbox from his father? What difference might it make in a spouse's ability to resist the temptations of a handsome colleague at work if her husband tells her each day how precious she is to him? What difference might it make in a single adult's courage to swim against the sexual tide of our culture if a female friend from the Christian community calls him to thank him for his faithfulness in serving others and in choosing God's purposes for his life? What difference might it make for a divorced person's rejection of the need to demonstrate his sexual prowess if a Christian brother and sister invite him to come to dinner and share his sorrow?

We see especially in all of these examples that the virtue of kindness is particularly valuable in the character of members of the Christian community in causing them to care more thoroughly about others in ways that will strengthen the others' ability to choose sexual behavior in accordance with God's design. We could also list many examples illustrating how the virtue of kindness in our own lives will cause our sexual behavior to be honorable and upbuilding and not manipulative or coercive.

Goodness

Closely related to kindness is the virtue of *agathōsynē*. This word is often used in the New Testament in a very general way to indicate a positive moral quality. At times the word is also used more particularly to indicate the act of generous giving that occurs in integral relationship with goodness. J. B. Phillips underscores this connotation when he renders the word "generosity" in his New Testament paraphrase.

It is extremely difficult to describe the virtue of goodness because the word is usually used in such a general way. My husband exemplifies this virtue to such a high degree that I am compelled (delightfully so!) to use him for an example. In fact, last week when I visited the school where he teaches, a few of his colleagues praised him to me using the expression, "Myron is so good." That word choice could have signified that Myron is skilled at teaching (which he is), but his friends meant instead that he is so morally upright. In atmospheres where there is often back-biting, jealousy, or other such nastinesses, the Christian virtue of goodness stands out as a noticeable alternative.

Goodness is a primary virtue for maintaining godliness in sexual behavior. Because of Myron's moral uprightness I never had to fear when we were single and best friends that he would violate God's standards — or mine or his. Perhaps we can also use the word *integrity* to describe this virtue.

Now that we are married and best friends, Myron's goodness is a constant strengthener of our union. It causes him to think more of others than of himself, and so his goodness begets all kinds of gracious actions (such as putting on my leg brace for me in the mornings when I'm not functioning well) that encourage me and bind us together. Moreover, his moral uprightness assures me that he will always keep clear the distinction between social and genital sexuality. Though he is very kind to all the women with whom he is associated at the elementary school, I know that his goodness keeps those relationships pure. Furthermore, that goodness is a strong means of social support for the "trampolines" of his colleagues.

Furthermore, the generosity of Myron's goodness toward many friends has shown me the importance in the Christian community of very practical acts of goodness to assist others in maintaining godly sexuality. For example, with the high cost of housing in many cities, it might be necessary in some instances for members of the Body to subsidize others to prevent single people from moving in together out of financial necessity. Another example is a very large congregation in a very small town that provides a place for pizza and root beer, fun and conversation for the town's youth after Friday night football games in order to keep them away from beer and "sex."

Notice again the importance of understanding these Spirit-produced virtues as both individual and corporate, as sources of both personal godliness in sexual matters and social support for others so that they can choose to live according to God's design. Because the moral integrity and gracious generosity of goodness are so comprehensive, the presence of this virtue in the fabric of personal character and in the quality of Christian community will create appealing alternatives to the sexual emptiness of our culture.

Faithfulness

In *A Community of Character,* Stanley Hauerwas suggests that the most important virtue necessary for marriage as a "heroic institution" is fidelity. Especially this virtue is vital as the Christian community offers alternatives because faithfulness is attacked by a culture that wants intensity rather than continuity,[6] momentary excitement rather than the long haul of relationship.

In a society in which the prevailing attitude is often "take 'em and leave 'em," the conscious choice to remain committed is a necessary imitation, as well as display, of God's faithfulness to humankind. Thus, this virtue ties in closely with the picture in Ephesians 5:21-33. The faithful submission and love of marriage partners makes visible the profound mystery of Christ's faithfulness to his Church.

6. Hauerwas, *A Community of Character* (Notre Dame: University of Notre Dame, 1981), p. 192.

The Greek term for this virtue, *pistis,* underscores the character strength of someone in whom complete confidence can be placed. Such a person is totally trustworthy and utterly dependable. The Jerusalem Bible's translation, "trustfulness," might suggest, moreover, that such a person is also more capable of trusting others.

Fidelity is especially a virtue of the long haul. It is difficult (though possible with repentance and forgiveness) to trust someone to be faithful to us in the future if that person has not been faithful in the past. Faithfulness for marriage, consequently, must begin in earliest childhood. It will cause youth to choose chaste behavior throughout adolescence because they want to be faithful to their future spouse.

Faithfulness is also an especially important gift in the Christian community so that its members can be more genuinely supportive of each other's social sexuality. I am convinced that many youth would refrain from becoming sexually active if they were more warmly welcomed, more strongly affirmed, and more affectionately cared for in the Body of Christ. The Church could also be a powerful agent in our world by modeling the delight of commitment in friendships that do not require genital sexual expression.

Gentleness

One aspect of the intertwining of these manifestations of the fruit of the Spirit that has not been previously noted is the way in which the various virtues prevent the others from degenerating into their negative extremes in the dialectics of human personality. Gentleness is an especially important example of this, particularly because of its place in the symbolically divine list of nine. Gentleness as a corollary prevents the previous virtue, faithfulness, from becoming austere as a burdensome duty or necessity. On the other side, gentleness protects the next virtue, self-control, so that it does not become rigid or inwardly proud and uncaring of others.

The Greek term, *praütēs*, includes both attitude and behavior and points positively to mildness or meekness. The latter words are often perceived by our "macho" culture as "wimpy" or "mousy," but the biblical notion emphasizes the strength of character necessary to deal gently with others.

Gentleness is especially known by its opposites. Louw and Nida note that the virtue is usually given in contrast to harshness, and they suggest that it might be translated with such idioms as "always speaking softly" or "not raising one's voice."[7] R. C. H. Lenski more fully observes that the opposite of gentleness is "to be arrogant, vehement, bitter, wild, and violent."[8] This list is especially helpful for pointing out the significant connection of gentleness with sexual behavior. In our society, so rife with sexual domineering, sexual abuse, promiscuity, harassment, rape, and sexual molestation, the Christian alternative of sexual gentleness is urgently needed and desired.

The Spirit-begotten virtue of gentleness will, by its courtesy and considerateness, protect the virginity of others. It will enable marriage partners to explore more carefully ways to please the other. It will foster a sense of beauty and purity in the gift of sexual union.

The virtue of gentleness is the only one in Paul's list that has a wide variety of translations, each of which captures aspects of the need for this virtue in sexual matters. The King James Version's rendering, "meekness," does not describe being a doormat but instead invites us into the mutual submission that Ephesians 5 commands. The translation in Today's English Version, "humility," counteracts

7. Louw and Nida, *Greek-English Lexicon*, vol. 1, p. 749.
8. Lenski, *The Interpretation of St. Paul's Epistles to the Galatians, Ephesians, and Philippians* (Minneapolis: Augsburg, 1937), p. 293.

our society's sexual pride and oppressing arrogance. J. B. Phillips's rendering, "tolerance," reminds us that spouses will gently accept the weaknesses of their marriage partners while working together to deepen their union.

Self-Control

We cannot really say that any of the virtues on Paul's list are any more important than the others for true obedience to the purposes of God in sexual matters, for they all undergird each other and are reinforced by the others. However, certainly self-control is extremely important for choosing God's design over the sexual values of our culture. In a society that propounds, "If it feels good, do it," it takes enormous courage and an act of will over one's emotions and instincts to choose to refrain from sexual intercourse outside the protective bonds of total commitment in marriage.

The Greek term, *enkrateia*, denotes exercising complete control over one's desires or actions. The thoroughness of this deliberate intentionality is conveyed well by the following set of ethnic idioms suggested for biblical translators by Louw and Nida: "to hold oneself in," "to command oneself," "to be a chief of oneself," "to make one's heart be obedient," "to command one's own desires," "to be the master of what one wants," or "to say No to one's body."[9]

The old King James Version's translation, "temperance," is inadequate to name this virtue because it might connote a modification of one's sexual desires rather than a complete mastery over them. We don't want compromise or a slight reduction; we want our Spirit-empowered sexual behavior to come entirely from a conscious choice to follow the instructions of the Designer and the model of Jesus.

9. Louw and Nida, *Greek-English Lexicon,* vol. 1, p. 752.

How timely (but extremely distressing!) that right at this point in my writing I just received an anonymous, sexually harassing phone call. What a shock! Such calls usually occur in the middle of the night and not in the bright morning. They graphically illustrate, as do the sexually explicit advertisements and films and the slang expressions of our times, how out of control our society is. Beset with fright after hanging up on the caller, I had to go around and secure the locks of my house. I wish my husband were home from school to protect me. I hate this sick feeling in the pit of my stomach. How destructive it is in our world that we women always have to be afraid for our sexual safety because our society is so out of control.

How precious is Spirit-bequeathed self-control. It is possible only in principled persons, for self-control must have a motivation, an ethical perspective, some overarching reasons by which we can get our bearings to make deliberate choices. We need a comprehensive narrative that instructs us in the way our will must choose to control our emotions and actions.

That is why the Christian community is so important for all that we have been discussing in this section. God's people have, since Abraham and Sarah, passed on the instructions, the stories, the blessings, and the promises that form us and nurture our characters so that we can reflect God's character. The narratives of the community give us the vision so that we can control the sinful nature in ourselves in order to choose instead the freedom of God's design for our lives. Self-control is not an onerous duty; rather, it is a Spirit-given discipline that sets us free to enjoy who we were really created to be.

The Trinity and the Virtues of Our Character

The symbolic nine are excellent representatives of all of the virtues that we want to learn from Jesus. Their grouping in three threes encourages us to think about the relationship of the Trinity[10] to these aspects of character, which will give rise to certain kinds of sexual behavior.

It seems to me that delight in choosing sexual carefulness is possible only for those who believe in a Creator whose design is so good that to choose it is most satisfying, and whose instructions fully guide us to live according to that design. Moreover, by the grace of Jesus, we know this Creator as Father.

I know that many theologians today argue that we should not use the term *Father* because it is oppressive to those who have been abused by their human fathers. I believe, to the contrary, that such people need more than anything to know God as "Father." By asserting this point I am *not* denying the need also to recover the feminine images for God in the Bible. However, our human psyches require both a mother and a father. If a person has been deprived of the security of a loving father's care, then the worst thing we can do is to take away from her any possibility for finding it. The best gift we can give is to introduce her to the true Father, the only one who can genuinely meet her needs for fathering. We can help her to acknowledge — and perhaps eventually to forgive — the failure of her human father to be the image of God he was designed to be. Most of all, we can demonstrate for her the true love of a real Father. Moreover, these gifts will

10. I am especially indebted to Professor Catherine LaCugna, who, during my graduate years at the University of Notre Dame, interested me in her powerful emphasis on the practicality of the doctrine of the Trinity. See Catherine Mowry LaCugna, *God for Us: The Trinity and Christian Life* (San Francisco: Harper, 1992).

benefit her own sexual identity and her ability to relate to men, especially socially, and eventually genitally.

Understanding the roles of the second person of the Trinity serves in several ways to develop our character for sexual godliness. Most important, Jesus is a tangible model to us of the virtues. The four Gospels give us many accounts that display Jesus' love, Joy, peace, patience, kindness, goodness, faithfulness, gentleness, and self-control, as well as many other virtues that will issue in chaste sexual behavior. We can explicitly see in him, furthermore, a model of relating to women with pure social sexuality rather than genital sexuality (contrary to what the film *The Last Temptation of Christ* would suggest!).

Furthermore, it is essential to know Jesus as Redeemer. Since he warns us that even to look lustfully at someone is to commit adultery (Matt. 5:27-28), we all have to admit to sexual sin. Certainly we must all confess regrets, mistakes, bad choices, fornications, adulteries, or misunderstandings of God's design. What good news it is that we are forgiven by the grace of Jesus Christ!

It is important that we announce this forgiveness especially to youth in our culture. Because many of them have been misled by the values that surround them in our society, once they hear of God's design they are often too overwhelmed with their past failures to choose it. Their attitude sometimes parallels that of a person who has cheated on her diet and therefore thinks she might as well go ahead and binge. We can often prevent future sexual misconduct if we enfold a person in God's forgiveness, to give him the courage to start again with better choices.

Finally, the Holy Spirit makes those new choices possible by empowering the godly, Christ-like life. It is VERY hard to choose God's design against the prevailing sexual mores of our world, but the Holy Spirit gives us the strength and courage to do so. It is VERY hard to be gentle in a violent world, to love with *agapē* in a self-centered world, to be master of oneself in a world that is out of control, but the Spirit creates virtues in us. The fruit of the Spirit in its various manifestations is all that we need to live with sexual purity and delight.

The first section of this book sketched a new basis for thinking about sexual ethics. This section has outlined the framework of that thinking. In Part III we will survey the kinds of questions we can be asking and some practical applications of this ethics to the phases of life and the issues of our times. Perhaps, though, before you move on, you might want to pause, as right now I feel compelled to do, to thank and praise God for all the gifts of the Trinity — for God's designing, creating, preserving, parenting, modeling, forgiving, revealing, instructing, and empowering.

III New Questions from an Ethics of Character for Practical Application to Issues of Our Day

"So choose life in order that you may live, you and your descendants, by loving the LORD your God, by obeying his voice, and by holding fast to him, for this is your life...."

DEUTERONOMY 30:19-20

8 *Friendship*

[handwritten: etc its loss in our culture]

When we ask what kind of people we need to be to uphold the vision for our sexuality laid out in the previous section of this book, we recognize immediately that a critical factor is the ability to distinguish between social and genital sexuality. We need to know how to establish and maintain relationships with diverse kinds of people to support our own "trampolines" of personal identity and to meet our needs for nongenital intimacy.

However, when we think about our technological society and how its toys and tools, its mobility and efficiency pull us away from each other, we sadly realize that such a world does not foster friendships or promote nongenital intimacy. In fact, many people in our society suffer from a severe lack of genuine friendship. They have great numbers of acquaintances and social contacts; they belong to numerous organizations or clubs; they participate in many social engagements and group activities. But they do not experience much opportunity for constructive intimacy or depth in personal relationships.

An easily observed indicator of the contemporary need for social intimacy is the kind of nostalgia and romantic sentiment that arises when we think about life before it became engulfed in the technological milieu. How I long for the comfortable serenity of my childhood family's summer evenings on the front porch swing when we talked with neighbors who were walking by. Many women remember friendly conversations over coffee or over the back fence. Couples often say to other couples, "We wish we could see you, but there isn't time right now." We have to schedule our moments together far in advance.

Much more is at stake, however, than simple nostalgia for less pressured and more friendly times. Our basic sense of sexuality is severely affected by myriads of factors in the technological milieu. For example, David F. Greenberg's massive historical and sociological study *The Construction of Homosexuality* shows how greatly such factors as urbanization and bureaucratization have affected the development of the modern homosexual identity.[1]

Greenberg's social-constructivist view forces the Church to ask better questions. How can we counteract our society's loss of communal guidance and lack of genuine friendship to be more helpful agents as the sexual identity of community members is formed? What alternative models can we offer the world for sexual understanding, for sexual chastity and fulfillment, for friendship?

Instead of challenging contemporary society's patterns, church leaders fall into our society's platitudes and behaviors. Especially troubling is not only the downfall of televangelists but also the dismissal of scholars in the academic world and professionals in churches because their inability to distinguish between social and genital sexuality has fostered actions which have led to charges against them by students and parishioners. Many persons who do not have the skill to form friendships are desperate for intimacy

1. Greenberg, *The Construction of Homosexuality* (Chicago: University of Chicago Press, 1988).

and reach for it in clumsy, deviant, manipulative, or oppressive ways.

Questions for the Christian Community

There are many ways in which the Christian community could offer our world help in the contemporary crisis of intimacy. I have dealt at length with how we could deepen the relationships of members within the Church in my previous book, *The Hilarity of Community*, so I need not discuss that here. It is important, however, to point out that relationships within the community are the place to start. In a great number of cases, churches don't have much to offer the society around them because they are not true communities themselves. Our congregations parallel the culture in techniques and pressures, in pushing for numbers instead of depth, in stifling friendship with busyness. If we want to reach out to our world with alternative models, therefore, our first task is to learn what it means genuinely to be the Church!

If we could truly be the Church, a Christian community in which we care for each other deeply and support each other's gifts and personhood, then we would offer to the world models of deep friendships built on the character, the faithfulness, of God. It is especially important that we ask in our churches what kind of persons we need to be, what virtues must be nurtured, and what we can do to foster and model all kinds of friendships — nongenital and honorable friendships across age, gender, social class, and racial lines.

The congregation to which Myron and I belong, for example, is beginning this year to use the Logos program for our midweek education. One of the great advantages of this program is that it involves so many of the adults of the congregation in its four components of play, study, meals, and worship skills. In all the interactions between persons of all ages the guiding rule is that we treat each other as children of God.

Last week as the first experience of the four-hour program unfolded, our pastor emphasized at dinner time how in our table manners we would especially remember that we were treating each other as the children of God. If someone spilled or knocked something over, we wouldn't say such rude things as "Were you born in a barn?" Instead, we would treat each other with encouragement and care. We also practiced such other courtesies as waiting until everyone was served before anyone began eating. What a superb way to nurture in both adults and children virtues of *agapē*, patience, kindness, goodness, and self-control — essential virtues for the formation of deep friendships.

One great advantage of this style of education is that the full program offers all of us the opportunity to become friends with people of various age levels — with the children with whom we work, with the other adults sharing in the tasks. My role is to serve as a table parent, and Myron helps the cleanup crew after dinner, after which we both head upstairs for the rehearsal of the choir, which I am directing this year. All three aspects give us different groups of people with whom we are becoming close. Since my customary work usually focuses on adults, I especially appreciate the chance to become friends with children of different ages; my table involves a high school student, three young teenagers, a ten-year-old, and an eight-year-old.

I hope that this particular program (one of many that congregations might choose) will challenge our congregation to ask some very important questions that are vitally necessary if we are going to be a community that fosters friendship. Which virtues especially must we nurture in children (and in ourselves!) so that we can be better friends? How could we structure the play times, the Bible study periods, the meal fellowships, and the practices for worship so that deeper relationships can be formed, so that intimacy can be graciously encouraged? How can we learn — and enable others — to express intimacy in wholesome, uplifting, nonthreatening, nonsuggestive ways? What are we doing to hold up the trampolines of everyone in our community? How, especially, are we welcoming the lonely and being friends with them?

There are numerous ways in which the Church can offer significantly alternative models to the society around us, but let us focus on three particularly important areas. The first is our friendship with the lonely or rebellious or marginalized. It takes hard work — and an enormous measure of the virtue of *agapē* — to befriend someone who lacks the skills to be a friend, to continue to care about someone who responds with coldness, distance, or even hostility. It requires patience to keep enfolding someone who doesn't know how to receive care because of tragic experiences or abuse. We need an extra measure of the virtues of goodness, kindness, and self-control to continue dealing graciously with someone who offends, exasperates, or hurts us.

One of the greatest assets that helps us to keep loving when it is hard to be a friend to someone is that we do not have to do it alone. We are part of a caring community, and together those of us in the Body encourage one another. For example, a victim of abuse needs to do a lot of talking to dump out the grief and confusion and fear. He requires a lot of support to learn to trust again. She must have constant enfolding to believe that God really does love. None of us could do alone all that the victim needs. But we can earnestly say, "Because I care about you so much, I don't want to try to hear your pain right now when I'm not able to listen any more. Your suffering is larger than just you and I, but other persons in the community will help us bear it," and then other members of the Body can continue the care.

A second important area in which the Church can offer a gift to our society is the area of young people's friendships. Not only can we give them specific guidance for developing nongenital relationships with their peers (to be discussed more thoroughly in Chapter 14 on teens and dating), but the Christian community can also be the context in which they can develop friendships with persons of all ages.

Besides teaching youth, through the narratives of the community, about *agapē* as a wonderful kind of love for satisfying our deepest needs to belong, congregational life can also foster deep friendships based on mutual interests *(philia)*. When we engage the youth in service projects, for example, they develop kinship bonds with those who share in the service. When they meet senior citizens of the congregation who take them under their wing because of common interests in fishing or building, crocheting or quilting, following the Chicago Cubs or myriads of other activities or crafts, the Church gives young people the great gift of mentors, confidantes, bosom buddies.

Moreover, when youth in the Body have multiple older friends, they have faithful people to turn to when they go through times of being at odds with their own parents. What spiritual and emotional support we can offer them when there are older sets of ears to hear their sorrows and love-tales — ears that are matched with compassionate hearts seeking God's best.

A third important dimension that we must reflect upon in our churches, as Stanley Hauerwas has pointed out, is how well we are affirming singleness as a legitimate form of living in the Christian community.[2] The biblical narratives (especially 1 Cor. 7) praise those who choose singleness for the sake of doing the work of the Kingdom. Many scoff at the urgency of the biblical descriptions and point out that, since Jesus did not come back as soon as everyone expected, these injunctions are therefore no longer relevant. On the contrary, the urgency is just as great now in the twentieth century as in the first, for we live in an un-Christian age, and the alternatives

2. Hauerwas, *A Community of Character* (Notre Dame: University of Notre Dame Press, 1981), p. 189.

of the Kingdom need to be proclaimed before we violent, greedy people destroy ourselves and the earth. There is still a great need for those who forego a marriage relationship because of the work to which God has called them.

For many years that seemed to be my calling, and in those single years the lack of support was very obvious to me. Why can't the Church be a place where single persons don't have to fear hearing unkind remarks — asking if they are married yet or wondering if there is something wrong with them because they are *still* single? Could not the Church — with *great* carefulness — take public notice of those who have chosen singleness for the sake of their ministries? I immediately think of several persons, both women and men, who, at the present time, are teachers, nurses, doctors, and youth workers — and would be immensely grateful for such affirmation of their service and single calling.

How can the Church also be a source of comfort and protection for those who are single not by choice? Many who have longed to be married have never had the opportunity; many struggle with personal handicaps or personality problems that seem to prohibit marriage. Some (it seems more often to be women) are strongly committed Christians who have never met an equally committed potential mate. Others have been deserted by a first spouse or have lost their partner to death. How are we upholding such persons? My participation in a task force for ministry to singles in the Lutheran Church taught me how rarely congregations reach out well to the many single persons in our society. Single persons compose forty percent of the population, but they certainly do not make up an equal proportion of the average congregation.

What should the Church do and be so that it is truly a family for single people, a haven of comfort for the lonely, a source of protection and provision for the widowed, a place where those who are alone can be appreciated and affirmed? It is especially important that we receive singles without dumping extra jobs on them because "they don't have family responsibilities and have more time." On the contrary, single people require extra time to balance home and work without the assistance of a spouse or children. On the other hand, sometimes singles who are eager to participate aren't asked to serve, for example, as greeters or coffee hosts, because they don't have an automatic "partner." In all cases, the community must be sensitive to each individual's need for solitude and companionship, for involvement according to the person's gifts, for support and encouragement.

Many church singles' groups degenerate into gatherings for spouse-hunting. How might congregations take care to create fellowships that nurture faith and godliness through Bible study and prayer, that foster nongenital friendships through shared activities and outreach, that provide places and times for conversation and mutual support?

Besides the frequent descriptions of godly virtues that will help to build strong friendships, the biblical narratives also give us guidance for our reflections on the subject through the accounts of many good models. Think, for example, about the friendships of Paul and Timothy (an intergenerational model), of Paul and Onesimus (a friendship across social classes and with an unbefriended other), of Jesus with Mary and with Martha (two very different nongenital, cross-gender friendships), and of Jesus and John (perhaps the epitome of a loving friendship).

What might be changed in your congregation so that it can become a caring community, a place of deep friendships across social, gender, and age differences? What virtues do we want to develop so that we can each be a better friend to those in our community? How can adults in our churches teach children the values and skills of friendship? How will the love in our communities enable us to reach beyond ourselves to be better friends to the world around us? What kind of people are we to be in order to model the friendship of God?

9 *Homosexuality*

This has been the most difficult chapter of the entire book to write, for the debates about homosexual behavior threaten to divide many church bodies and alienate many people on both sides of the issue. Especially distressing is the violence manifested both by those who believe that homosexual behavior should be accepted by the Church and by those who claim that the Bible forbids such activity.

Because our concern in this book is for the character of God's people, we recognize immediately that such violence and hostility are contrary to the virtues of the Kingdom of God. Therefore, we want to enter into the debates about homosexuality with the utmost patience and gentleness and love.

What Questions Must We Ask?

The debates in the Church about homosexual behavior become especially murky often because we fail to ask clear questions and keep the discussion focused on one dimension of the problem at a time. Of course, all of the issues cannot be neatly divided, but it is particularly helpful if we separate exegetical from hermeneutical questions — that is, questions about what the texts in the Bible actually say and questions about how to apply the Scriptures to contemporary life. If our careful study of biblical perspectives is mixed with personal opinions and experiences, we wind up with fruit compote and are not able to assess distinctly the quality of the apples and oranges by themselves.

Because we are attempting in this book to sketch an approach to ethical issues based on the character of the Church, our methodological order is significant. As previously discussed, we who desire to be followers of Jesus are different from the world around us insofar as our lives are formed by the revelation of God's design for humankind. Therefore, our first step in pursuing any ethical matter is to discern as clearly as possible what God says in his Word. Because there is much confusion in the Church on the subject of homosexuality, we will have to spend much more time than usual in this chapter ferreting out the truths of the biblical revelation. Once we know what God says, then we can ask better questions about how the Scriptural accounts apply to our concern and care for homosexuals in the twentieth century.

What Does the Bible Actually Say?

Of the many articles and books written to guide the Church in the difficult matter of how to accept homosexuals, Richard B. Hays's article "Relations Natural and Unnatural: A Response to John Boswell's Exegesis of Romans 1" in *The Journal of Religious Ethics* stands out because Hays, a New Testament scholar then at Yale University and now at Duke, carefully separates the issues for more accurate analysis.[1]

---

1. Hays, "Relations Natural and Unnatural: A Response to John

Since it is impossible to detail all of this superb article here, I encourage all of those who are concerned about the ongoing debates in various church bodies to read it, especially because Hays responds to John Boswell's *Christianity, Social Tolerance, and Homosexuality,*[2] which has widely impacted those debates (211).[3] Out of his deep concern for the false weight that Boswell's exegesis has had in churches, Hays argues that "he not only misconstrues the Romans text, but also fosters an unfortunate confusion between exegesis and hermeneutics" (185).

First of all, Hays takes the critically important step, neglected by many who deal with the difficult Romans 1 passage about homosexuality, of studying the text in its context. Hays is certainly right to recognize that Romans 1:26-27 cannot be understood apart from the unfolding logic of Paul's whole argument in Romans 1. He outlines two major thrusts in that chapter — "the keynote of the Gospel: the righteousness of God" (emphasizing God's jus-

---

Boswell's Exegesis of Romans 1," *The Journal of Religious Ethics* 4, 1 (Spring 1986): 184-215. Page references to this article in the rest of this chapter will be given parenthetically in the text.

2. Boswell, *Christianity, Social Tolerance, and Homosexuality* (Chicago: University of Chicago Press, 1980). See also the following, which do not respond to Boswell but present careful biblical perspectives: "The Law of Holiness: Leviticus 18-20," chapter 7 in Walter C. Kaiser's *Toward Old Testament Ethics* (Grand Rapids: Academie Books, 1983); Greg L. Bahnsen's *Homosexuality: A Biblical View* (Grand Rapids: Baker Book House, 1978); and David Field's *The Homosexual Way — A Christian Option* (Downers Grove, IL: InterVarsity Press, 1979).

3. Boswell's impact came largely before his book was published through the influence of his manuscript on John J. McNeil's *The Church and the Homosexual* (Kansas City: Sheed, Andrews, and McMeel, 1976) and, through McNeil, on James B. Nelson's *Embodiment: An Approach to Sexuality and Christian Thought* (Minneapolis: Augsburg Publishing House, 1978) and on *Is the Homosexual My Neighbor?* (New York: Harper & Row, 1978) by Letha Scanzoni and Virginia Ramey Mollenkott.

tice and integrity) and "God's wrath revealed: unrighteousness rampant" (showing how Rom. 1:18-32 "explains, documents, and elaborates" the unrighteousness of human beings). The critical element to note — which parallels this book's emphasis on sexual behaviors as idolatry — is that all depravities follow from the radical rebellion of human beings against their Creator. Hays concludes that "the passage is not merely a polemic denunciation of selected pagan vices; it is a diagnosis of the human condition" (190).

Robin Scroggs uses the fact that homosexual behavior is only of secondary and illustrative importance in Paul's argument to lessen its normative force,[4] but Hays contends that it is an illustration particularly vivid to Paul and his readers. As Victor Furnish has made clear, in the first century after Christ there was an emerging negative consensus concerning homosexual practice throughout the cultural environment, not only among Jews and Christians, but also among popular pagan moral philosophers.[5] He contends that "to discerning ethical teachers in the Greco-Roman world it seemed just as obvious that homosexual practices were necessarily exploitative as that they were inevitably born of insatiable lust."[6] Therefore, according to Hays, "Paul's choice of homosexuality as an illustration of human depravity is not merely random; it serves his rhetorical purposes by providing a vivid *image* of humanity's primal rejection of the sovereignty of God the creator" (191).

It is not necessary to sketch here Hays's comments about Paul's rhetorical devices and conventions (191-95), but we should especially notice the cleverness of Paul's

---

4. Scroggs, *The New Testament and Homosexuality* (Philadelphia: Fortress Press, 1983), pp. 113-14.

5. Furnish, *The Moral Teaching of Paul* (Nashville: Abingdon Press, 1979), pp. 52-83.

6. Furnish, *The Moral Teaching of Paul,* p. 67.

rhetorical trap in Romans 2:1, which catches every reader in the recognition that *all* human beings stand equally under the just judgment of a righteous God. We will note in the second-to-last section of this chapter the significance of this trap; we cannot read about homosexual practices in Paul without remembering his admonition to everyone.

Hays next develops his exegetical work by responding specifically to Boswell. He summarizes thus:

> In the context of Paul's exposition, the reference to homosexual behavior functions as *prima facie* evidence of the moral confusion and blindness which has come upon the human race as a result of its refusal to acknowledge God the creator. (195)

Hays criticizes Boswell and others who want to apply in their exegesis the modern idea of a permanent homosexual orientation being natural. It is an anachronism to suggest that Paul had in mind the modern notion of a "gay" constitution. Instead, he clarifies that the apostle Paul's charge

> that these fallen humans have "exchanged natural relations for unnatural" means nothing more nor less than that human beings, created for heterosexual companionship, as the Genesis story bears witness, have distorted even so basic a truth as their sexual identity by rejecting the male and female roles which are "naturally" theirs in God's created order. (200)

Though the brief sketch of Hays's argument here cannot convey adequately its thoroughness, his exegesis convincingly displays that "in Romans 1:26-27 we find an unambiguous indictment of homosexual behavior as a violation of God's intention for humanity" (205).[7] The difficult ques-

---

7. We find a similarly unambiguous indictment of homosexual

tion is what that means for the attitudes and perceptions of the twentieth-century Church.

A Hermeneutical Excursus

Many commentators simply suggest that Paul's passage was a corrective text for his time that is no longer culturally relevant, now that we know so much more about homosexuality. Lest the Church accept that move too readily, we must sidetrack to consider the different types of passages in the Scriptures. Basically we must distinguish three major kinds as follows:

(A) normative or instructive texts — those which give basic, fundamental principles that should characterize the people of God;

(B) descriptive texts — those which narrate examples of practices acceptable and unacceptable among the people of God and their results;

(C) problematic or corrective texts — those which deal with specific problems among the Jews or in the early Church.

Those who want to discard Romans 1 because it is a type C kind of text fail to place it in its entire context as does Hays. A slight excursus here will make the falsity of that hermeneutical move more evident.

---

behavior in the First Testament. The warning against male-male intercourse in Leviticus 18:22 is part of a long series of actions — such as incest, child sacrifice, and oppression of the poor — which are condemned by God because they "pollute the land" (or, in the language of this book, they spoil God's design). Similarly, the same description of homosexual action in Leviticus 20:13 is part of another list of practices — including adultery, incest, and bestiality — which are to be severely punished because they hurt the family.

Many passages in the Bible are clearly type C texts and for various reasons cannot be normatively applied to later generations. One example might be the admonitions for women to wear veils or not to wear pearls or braided hair. Since diverse cultural times and places call for different dress to indicate chastity, these requirements wouldn't easily transfer to another era.

Other corrective passages (type C) are not transferable because they are not congruent with the main thrust of the gospel. When they seem to conflict with a principle (type A) and/or with the biblical examples (type B) because they deal exclusively with a particular problem in a specific situation, then we must find out why the situation of the type C text called forth such a correction. For example, the admonition in 1 Corinthians 14:34 for women not to speak contradicts normative passages (type A) about gifts and descriptive passages (type B) of women serving in leadership positions. The close context of 1 Corinthians 14:33-35 and the whole discourse of 1 Corinthians 11–14 enable us to see that the issue was simply the particular problem of disorderly chatter, which could be easily solved if women asked husbands their questions at home.[8] Such a corrective text should not be turned into a normative principle, as many churches did — and still do.

Other corrective passages are perfectly congruent with other normative and descriptive texts. These corrective texts border on the normative because they are not culture specific and because they are congruent with the whole of Scripture. Corrective passages about homosexuality fit into this category because they are congruent with the normative texts about God's design for sexual union and with the

8. For a more thorough consideration of this hermeneutical problem, see my essays "Hermeneutical Considerations for Biblical Texts" and "I Timothy 2:8-15," in *Different Voices/Shared Vision*, ed. Paul Hinlicky (Delhi, NY: American Lutheran Publicity Bureau, 1992), pp. 15-24.

descriptive texts that display negative consequences for violations of that design.[9] "The witness of Scripture is univocal," Richard Hays observes. "Whatever one may decide about the weight of the appeal to the love-principle, however, the fact remains that no biblical text directly contradicts the authority of Paul's teaching on this matter" (208).

Moreover, Paul's argument in Romans 1 has also provided the grounding for the continuing tradition of the Church. A historical overview reveals that

> every pertinent Christian text from the pre-Constantinian period . . . adopts an unremittingly negative judgment on homosexual practice, and this tradition is emphatically carried forward by all major Christian writers of the fourth and fifth centuries. (202)

We must ask, then, what bearing this normative/corrective tradition in Scripture and in the early Church has on twentieth-century deliberations.

How Does the Bible Apply?

Richard Hays lays out the question well in the following summary:

> Given the fact that Paul, in common with every other early Christian writer who addressed the issue, apparently regarded all homosexual activity as immoral, we still have to decide how to construe the authority of his

9. In the cases of the two descriptive passages of homosexual behavior in Genesis 19 and Judges 19 (which contain many parallels), the actions are described with strong verbs which suggest that those wanting sexual relations with the male guests would even break down the doors in order to "know" them. Homosexual relations are named "evil," "impious," "wanton," "disgraceful."

opinion in the present time. Because there remain open questions about precisely *how* the Bible functions as an authority for normative ethical judgments, we cannot relieve ourselves of the responsibility for moral decision by appealing to the plain sense of a single prooftext; nor, on the other hand, should we feel constrained to force Paul, through exegetical contortions, to say what we think he ought to have said. We must let the text have its say, whether for us or against us; then we must decide what obedience to God requires. (205)

Hays's discussion of the problems of applying texts to our times is guided by these two questions:

1. What is the mode or level of discourse in which the text may appropriately function as a source of appeal for normative judgments?
2. How is the text to be coordinated with or weighed against other authorities? (205)

Again, we cannot thoroughly replay here Hays's entire discussion, though his carefulness is exemplary. Surveying five categories for moral application proposed by James Gustafson, Hays insists that the fourth, "Understanding of the World and Humankind," is

the mode in which Romans 1 speaks; it offers an analysis of humankind in rebellion against God and consequently plunged into depravity and confusion. In the course of the analysis, homosexual activities are — explicitly and without qualification — identified as symptomatic of that tragically confused rebellion. Thus, it is possible and methodologically appropriate to take Paul's account, both in general and with regard to its particulars, as "revealed reality"; an authoritative depiction of the human condition. The text then would inform a normative evaluation of homosexual practice as a distortion of God's order for creation. (206-7)

Hays also recognizes that the text functions, in Gustafson's fifth category, to develop "Understanding of God." As such, Romans 1 does not reveal patterns in the character of God that human beings can emulate, but God's righteousness and wrath and mercy motivate our ethical responses. Finally, Hays comes to this conclusion:

> Thus, Romans 1 confronts us with an account of how the ordering of human life before God has gone awry. To use the text appropriately in ethical reflection about homosexuality, we should not try to wring laws or principles or analogies out of it. If Romans 1 is to function appropriately to inform normative ethical judgments about homosexuality, it must function as a diagnostic tool, laying bare the truth about humankind's dishonorable "exchange" of the natural for the unnatural; according to Paul, homosexual relations, however they may be interpreted (or rationalized — cf. Romans 1:32) by fallen and confused creatures, represent a tragic distortion of the created order. (Obviously, this judgment leaves open many questions about how best to deal with the problem pastorally.) Do we grant the normative force of Paul's analysis? (207)

That final question is the one that has frequently been ignored in discussions that mix exegesis and hermeneutics. If what the Bible says is not so carefully explicated, then the need for determining if we will admit it as normative is not so stark. Our church bodies must be very clear. What sources of authority are relevant to our discussions about homosexuality?

The ensuing discussion (207-9) in Hays's article about Scripture, tradition, reason, and experience as sources of authority makes definitively clear the essence of the whole debate in the Church about homosexual practice. The conflicts arise because homosexuals in our era now claim that in their stable and loving relationships they experience the grace of God. How should we assess such claims? As throughout this chapter, Hays poses the question better than I can:

> Was Paul wrong? Or are such experiential claims simply another manifestation of the blindness and self-deception that Paul so chillingly describes? . . . Or are there new realities that Paul didn't know about?

Many modern writers claim the latter, that God is "doing a new thing," as Isaiah promised. Instead of anachronistically imposing modern ideas on ancient texts, we must recognize the real collision between their respective worldviews. Robin Scroggs, for example, acknowledges that various New Testament passages, including 1 Corinthians 6:9 and 1 Timothy 1:10, condemn homosexual activity, but he denies that those texts can be applied directly to the contemporary situation.[10]

Similarly, a 1992 Society of Biblical Literature panel, discussing homosexuality as "A Case Issue in the Use of Biblical Authority," found several ways to circumvent the texts. One panelist suggested that, just as Paul set aside Israelite food purity laws for the sake of the unity of the Church, so we should now for unity's sake set aside sexual purity laws. Such a suggestion ignores the congruity of the biblical texts about homosexual practice with all normative and descriptive passages about God's design for sexuality.

As debates about homosexual behavior rage on, Hays's concluding remarks set out clearly these basic choices that lie before the Christian community:

10. Scroggs, *The New Testament and Homosexuality*, pp. 123-29.

101

Romans 1 should decisively undercut any self-righteous condemnation of homosexual behavior. Those who follow the church's tradition by upholding the authority of Paul's teaching against the morality of homosexual acts must do so with due humility. . . .

Likewise, those who decide that the authority of Paul's judgment against homosexuality is finally outweighed by other considerations ought to do so with a due sense of the gravity of their choice. The theological structure in which Paul places his indictment of relations "contrary to nature" is a weighty one indeed, and it is not explicitly counterbalanced by anything in Scripture or in Christian tradition. Arguments in favor of acceptance of homosexual relations find their strongest warrant in empirical investigation and in contemporary experience. Those who defend the morality of homosexual relationships within the church may do so only by conferring upon these warrants an authority greater than the direct authority of Scripture and tradition. . . .

Only when the issue is posed in these terms does the painful difficulty of the decision become clear. . . . We must forthrightly recognize that in Romans 1 Paul portrays homosexual activity as a vivid and shameful sign of humanity's confusion and rebellion against God; then we must form our moral choices soberly in light of that portrayal. (210-11)

How Should the Church Respond?

I have given such a thorough overview of Hays's article because it makes more clear than anything else I've found on the subject exactly what issues are at stake in the denominational debates about homosexual practice, and yet it has not been widely disseminated in the Church. Now we can test what our ethics of sexual character might say in response to Hays's stark proposal of the "painful difficulty of the decision." What kinds of questions will we ask, guided by our concern for the virtues and for God's design for humanity?

Because of our emphasis on character, we immediately recognize that much more gentleness and compassion are required in dealing with the issues. We cannot join with those who affirm the biblical picture in ways that are hostile to persons of homosexual orientation.[11] Because scientific research about the modern idea of constitutional homosexuality is still in process,[12] those of us who are heterosexual cannot really understand the situation of those who are, or claim to be, homosexual by nature.

Tragically, Christians do not demonstrate the virtues of Christ when they stigmatize homosexuals as terribly despicable sinners. Boswell's study fully displays how, throughout history, much of Christian ethical teaching has been relentlessly hostile to homosexual behavior.

Hays, in the course of his argument, offers a good model for the character with which this topic must be discussed. He insists that

> the expression "contrary to nature" probably did not carry for Paul and his readers the vehement connotation of "monstrous abomination" which it subsequently acquired in Western thought about homosexuality. Consequently, this phrase should certainly not be adduced as if it were a biblical warrant for the frantic homophobia which sometimes prevails in modern society. (199)

11. Violence surrounded a recent Oregon ballot anti-gay-rights measure, which was defeated; a passed measure in Colorado is leading to increased "gay bashing."
12. Research that detected differences in the brain structure of homosexuals has been called into question by the fact that all the subjects tested died of AIDS. It has not been determined if AIDS or homosexuality caused the brain structure differences.

How can we in the Church better counteract the homophobia that erupts in church bodies and in the society around us? What opportunities can we provide for listening better to the concerns of homosexuals, for caring for the needs of those suffering with AIDS, for building friendships across the barriers between homosexuals and heterosexuals?

On the other hand, if we in the Christian community claim to be formed by the revelation of God rather than by human delusions and confusions, then we must recognize that the phrase "contrary to nature" does depict homosexual unions as opposed to the design of God. This is evidenced simply by the fact that it is impossible for such acts to "bear fruit and multiply," as is the nature of heterosexual unions. Consequently, because of these clear scriptural assertions, our communities ask homosexuals in our midst to remain celibate.

If we recognize sexual intercourse as God's sign for permanent, committed marriage relationships, does not any other involvement in sexual union — whether by heterosexuals or by homosexuals — lie outside of that design? In order to help each member of the Church preserve the distinction between genital and social sexuality, and to prevent rebellious sexual union, how can our communities do a better job of supporting each individual's trampoline with genuine friendship and love?

To accept homosexual *persons* is certainly part of the task of the Christian community in caring for each other — but we must recognize that the continued call for acceptance in the Church of homosexual *sexual activity* manifests instead the persistent sexual idolatry of this age. Furthermore, that idolatry is presently forcing many church bodies to push for a "new hermeneutic" based on a "love-principle" that distorts the genuine *agapē* we have defined in this book. Various groups suggest that the "loving" thing to do is to accept homosexual unions or that homosexual behavior which is "loving" or nonexploitative is not what Leviticus and Romans 1 condemn. Richard Hays reacts to this movement as follows:

> I would suggest that if we are in a new hermeneutical situation, it is not primarily because we know something that Paul did not know about "sexology"; rather, it is because prevailing social attitudes have changed so that the value-neutral ideal of empirical investigation has tacitly come to acquire near-normative force in the formation of popular moral judgments about sexual behavior. (214)

If we are a community formed by God's revelation, then we give primary authority to the texts of the Scriptures and not to the experience of certain persons — always remembering that those texts of Scripture stand in judgment over all of us.

But Is It Fair?

During workshops on sexuality, when I share both my concern for homosexual persons and my desire to be faithful to God's Word and its call for celibacy, the response frequently is, "But that isn't fair. What gives the Church the right to deny homosexuals any possibility for sexual fulfillment?"

That question is an excellent one for several reasons. First of all, it points up again the sexual idolatry of our times — that it seems as if the Christian community is doing persons the greatest possible injustice if we deny them the opportunity for sexual involvement. Why do we make "sex" so important?

Second, the question should be turned on its head and directed to the Christian community. Why are we not more

105

supportive of the social sexuality of persons, why are we not better friends, so that the desperation for genital satisfaction is not so strong? Why have we not more thoroughly developed in the Christian community an awareness that, in contrast to the notion of our society, the human will is stronger than emotions or passions/lusts and that we who choose the designs of God can help each other have the courage to act out of will rather than sexual desire? Why do we not display better models of deep, same-gender, nongenital friendships to enable homosexuals to resist the imperative for genital fulfillment in our culture?

Moreover, David Greenberg's study *The Construction of Homosexuality* has confirmed my long-standing belief that many persons in our culture become convinced that they are homosexual because the sociological category is so prevalent and openly affirmed.[13] Yearnings for friendship and simple childhood experimentation are misconstrued,

13. Greenberg, *The Construction of Homosexuality* (Chicago: University of Chicago Press, 1989). Greenberg's massive historical and sociological study disproves the contemporary notion of an essential/natural static homosexuality as a biological condition or psychological orientation. His almost 300-page overview of sexual patterns, behaviors, and ideas before modern times demonstrates instead that sexual identity is formed and interpreted by different cultures in various ways. His general typology of homosexualities in primitive and archaic societies — transgenerational, transgenderal, egalitarian, initiation-rite, cultic, and class-structured homosexualities — displays an enormous range of examples against which the idea of a static homosexual essence cannot stand.

Then, in the book's second part, Greenberg discusses thoroughly how the modern social classification has created both the modern homosexual identity and the evaluative framework by which to judge it on the spectrum of deviant to admirable — and generally now with more tolerance. Different factors of the milieu's social logics nurture present developments — urbanization erodes communal guidance; science leads to deterministic thinking; the medicalization of homosexuality has developed many theories of its origin; and bureaucratization depersonalizes social controls based on family and community.

but they might be labeled differently if so many forces in our society wouldn't favor the development of homosexual character. Once the suspicion is planted, then repeated behaviors reinforce that orientation. Our ethics of character has to ask how the Church might instead model and foster upbuilding, nongenital, same-gender friendships, and how we could more positively assist young people in discovering their sexual identity according to God's created design. How might our deep, personal friendships with and counsel for homosexuals relieve their pressure to prove themselves sexually?[14]

Third, the question of "fairness" raises the whole issue of suffering. When I ask homosexuals for celibacy, I am not asking anything more of them than I asked of myself all the years that I was single. Celibacy was a good (but sometimes painfully difficult) choice for me in order to be faithful to the purposes of God. How can the Christian community make God's purposes for bringing the Kingdom to bear on all aspects of our world more important to homosexuals so that they can choose it gladly and forego genital fulfillment?

Fourth, the question is often expanded with words such as these: "But homosexuals can't help it that they are gay. So it isn't fair to deny them sexual pleasure." This aspect of the question causes me the most anguish, because I recognize that various social factors, environmental causes, and perhaps heredity (since science hasn't discovered all the reasons) do bring about homosexuality in persons against their will. Many whom I have counseled confess that they have tried all kinds of programs to

14. I ask this because one homosexual I counseled said that he knew he was gay because he had "tried sex with a woman and it wasn't very satisfying." We know that such an experience rips sexual union out of context and so wouldn't be satisfying for heterosexuals either. Another counselee found her suspicions of lesbianism groundless when she rightly named her childhood experimentation.

change, have trusted God to change them, have prayed for change, and so forth, but still find themselves sexually attracted to persons of the same gender. How can the Church find ways to be more sensitive to this acute suffering?

Perhaps my physical handicaps make me more aware of the true nature of the questions — or perhaps they make me more blunt. I can't help but respond to the question of fairness by asking in turn, "Is it fair that I who once was extremely active and skilled in sports am denied the physical pleasure of running and playing because of a crippled leg? Is it fair that, loving music as profoundly as I do, I am denied the sensual pleasure of hearing it well because my deaf ear constantly rings? Is it fair that severe visual limitations prevent me from enjoying beauty and make me unable to do the reading that I love and must do for my work?" To be denied sexual fulfillment (as I also was for many single years) does not seem to me to be such a great suffering. Though I am passionately in love with my husband, I would gladly give up sexual happiness to get my vision back. (You see, my dear reader, I am easily as guilty of making an idol of visual pleasure as others might be of the idolatry of sexual pleasure. We are all sinners in rebellion against our Creator!)

I have thought and prayed repeatedly about taking out the previous paragraph, but I can't. It states — perhaps too starkly — the crux of the matter. We live in a broken world, filled with suffering of all sorts. Most of our suffering comes to us against our will, and then it is up to us to decide how to respond to it. I can wallow in my physical limitations and throw pity parties, or I can "seize the day" and use whatever is left to serve God's purposes. Those who are homosexual suffer greatly because their desires do not match God's design for sexuality. They have the choice to rebel against their Creator (who is not to blame for their orientation — his creation design is clearly for male/

female unions) or to submit to his will for their sexual celibacy. It is not too great a suffering to ask of homosexuals that they remain celibate for the sake of the Kingdom of God. All of us have to bear certain sufferings in this broken and sinful world. And the grace of God makes them all bearable, whether they are physical, sexual, or other.

How can our Christian communities be more supportive of homosexuals as they bear the suffering of sexual celibacy? Even more important, how can we stop causing them other kinds of suffering — by our misunderstandings, our labels, our failures to listen, our inability to see that homosexual orientation is not sin and that we, too, are tempted to rebel against God's designs for celibacy and genital purity? All of us are sinners worthy of God's judgment and yet receiving grace instead through Jesus Christ.

This chapter is intended to guide the Church's theology and practice. It is not written to suggest how we might talk with homosexuals personally. We dare not self-righteously "dump the truth" on them. Rather, we who care about them in the Christian community must spend time with them gently to encourage their choice of God's will for their sexuality, to stand by them and forgive their rebellions, to apologize for the pain we cause them, to support their personhood and gifts, to resist with them the cultural notion that we are not complete without genital fulfillment. Only if we all acknowledge our complicity in sin — in sexual or other idolatries and rebellions against our Creator — do we have anything to say.

e.g. the R.C. nun who boasted femininity without genital intimacy! Still female! Still male!

10 *Marriage*

Today is our "dies-versary"! Myron and I have been married exactly three years, three months, and nineteen days. I celebrated by putting a love note in his lunch bag. Myron brought in for me a lovely lavender rose from the garden.

"Mo-versaries" are even more special — I try to have a little present or a card for Myron each month — and, of course, the "anni-versaries" are major holidays because we are so grateful for each year we are given together. Probably we are more aware than most couples of the preciousness of our days and months together because we know that they will most likely be limited. (Taking the best care possible, I'm praying to continue to outlive the doctors' expectations.) Sometimes people tell us that if we had been married for many years, we wouldn't be so enamored with each other, but I wonder. Does marriage have to get stale?

It seems to me that keeping a marriage alive is very much like keeping myself alive. The three main ingredients are a reason for living, intense self-discipline, and, most important, the grace of God. Exploring this analogy will give us directions for the Church's task of nurturing per-

110

sonal virtues and character to build healthier marriages in our Christian communities.

Marriage Goals

First of all, a marriage cannot exist very well just for itself — and certainly not just for the sexual fulfillment of the marriage partners. If it is too "inward-turned" (as Martin Luther would say), a relationship suffocates the partners instead of liberating them. As we learned in Part II, Christian marriage exists above all to symbolize the mystery of God's faithfulness to his people. That reason to live gives marriage a profound motivation, and such a goal makes the required effort enormously worthwhile.

My personal handicaps teach me the importance of having worthwhile goals. There are times when all the chores of staying alive get really tiresome — multiple insulin injections and blood test pokes, eight kinds of medications to counteract various debilitations, hundreds of laser burns and occasional surgeries to save vision, surgeries to unknot my hands, always wearing a leg brace, being in a wheelchair right now because of slow-healing wounds on both feet, constant infection battles, daily exercise workouts however I feel, endless trips to doctors and specialists, chronic and sometimes overwhelming pain. What makes the routines and disciplines worthwhile are all the goals that stand before me — books to write, ideas to teach, projects to undertake, music and beauty to enjoy, Myron to love.

The tasks and attitudes necessary for keeping a Christian marriage alive are magnificently worthwhile because of the preeminence of the goals. If our human unions have the privilege of demonstrating the faithfulness of God, such a profound motivation enables us to decide before we ever enter into marriage that this WILL be permanent. Conflicts

111

and confusions will end in resolution and repentance and reconciliation, not rupture. How could there be an end to God's loyalty and constant love? We are challenged to live accordingly.

This goal raises several important questions for the Christian community's work of nurturing its young people in preparation for marriage. How can we help children realize that the goal of symbolizing God's fidelity by our own sexual faithfulness gives us sufficient motivation for taming our unruly sexual desires? In her diatribes against the Presbyterian sexuality study (discussed in Chapter 4), Camille Paglia's comment that the report did not take into consideration the lusts of human nature demonstrates the modern notion that feelings are stronger than will. Of course, we all have to battle strong sexual desires that tempt us to rebel against the Creator's intentions for genital expression only within the framework of a marriage's permanent commitment, but the goal of symbolizing God's faithfulness gives us ample resources for overcoming impulse with intentional purpose.

How can we help our children, from their earliest awareness, to discover the delight of God's design for permanence in marriage? We will not speak of it lightly. We will point the children to models of solid, long-term marriages — not at all suggesting that those couples are perfect in their life together, but pointing out that they are faithful. As a congregation, how might we make a big deal out of celebrating anniversaries? We could pray with gratitude for them in public worship services, list them in the monthly newsletter, give parties for the major ones — or whatever else will demonstrate in our rituals the great value of faithfulness. How can we teach our children patience? How shall we combat our society's requirement of immediate gratification, so that our children are able to wait until they find a marriage partner with whom they can build a lasting union?

The goal of demonstrating the permanence of God's love and grace also gives the Church many guidelines for its encouragement of couples. How can we support the delight of marriage partners in each other — perhaps most importantly by not pulling them away from each other, as congregations often do? Can we keep the mechanics of a congregation to a minimum so that couples are freed from onerous committee responsibilities that become too burdensome? I am talking here not about legitimate avenues of service that use their gifts but about tiresome tasks that merely aggravate their busyness. Do we foster a Sabbath day of delight for spouses, or do we fill their Sundays up with meetings? Do we promote such events as marriage enrichment weekends or couples retreats or other activities that focus on nourishing faithfulness?

A second goal in Christian marriage is to raise children in a way that passes on to the next generation the traditions of the faith. We will explore that particular aspect more thoroughly in Chapter 12, "Nurturing Children," but it is important at this point to notice how such a goal is effective for sustaining marriage (though it is not sufficient, as evidenced by the many divorces that occur when the nest becomes empty). If marriage partners realize that they are signs to their family of the fidelity and grace of God and agents for nourishing their children's glad response to that grace, they are greatly encouraged in their faithfulness to each other and in more faithful imaging of God's parenting for their children.

This goal, too, gives specific guidance for the Christian community, as will be discussed in Chapter 12. Furthermore, it also relates to the debates about abortion, because the recognition that Christian marriages raise children to carry on the faith has great implications for the question of how we welcome children into the world. We will look at these implications more closely in Chapter 13.

Another goal in Christian marriage is for the couple to

113

be strengthened by their union to reach out beyond themselves to others. Thus, marriage is viewed not only as a delight in itself but also as a springboard for service. In order for the congregation to foster this attitude and support its couples in it, we must ask critical questions about how thoroughly our community is calling forth the gifts of its members, how well we avoid imposing false pressures on persons to contribute service not according to their gifts, how much we encourage contributions to society by the members of the Body. For example, do our congregations sponsor couples' Bible studies so that spouses can search the Scriptures together and be supported by the prayers and affirmations of other group members in offering their gifts of service to the world?

A fourth goal for Christian marriage (among many others that we could discuss) is that a union in Christ is both a source and a sign of hope. This goal is closely related to the first, because hope is grounded, not in circumstances, but in the fidelity of God. Because our marriage is founded on the promise of a permanent covenant, the assurance of Myron's faithfulness gives me hope no matter what complications my body develops, and Myron's confidence in my commitment gives him hope in the face of the difficulties of teaching elementary school. Moreover, our belief in God's provision for our future together, no matter what things might go wrong, can be a sign of hope to those around us. In the midst of a world characterized by violence, unfaithfulness, economic chaos, and suffering of all sorts, Christian marriages boldly declare that the sovereign God is in control of the future and therefore can be trusted to lead us through the present.

How can our Christian communities better foster such an awareness in the members of the Body? One problem that I have observed in many churches around the country is that worship services are not nurturing hope. This is another topic, too large to deal with adequately here, but the contemporary tendency to focus on subjective feelings about God rather than on the character and intervention of God precludes the development of genuine hope. Both music and sermons often fail to proclaim the truth about God, to paint a picture of God's future in order to inspire hope for the present, to invite worshipers into the biblical vision. Our worship practices develop character, and a hopeful character is an essential part of marriage — both as a gift we bring to each other to sustain us in our union and as a gift we offer to the world by means of our union.

These four goals are prime examples, to which we could add particular goals specific to each marriage, which give the partners courage and grit, motivation and sustenance for practicing the personal and mutual disciplines necessary to maintain a vital marriage. How can our churches help members, especially young people and married couples, to accept and live by these goals? Once, after giving a Sunday homily on Genesis 2 and God's design for Christian marriage, I was totally astounded by how many people said that they had never heard such a message before in a worship service. In a society that is bombarding us with opposing views, we cannot take for granted that believers know the biblical vision. How can we more specifically, more frequently, and more fervently paint the picture? We do not have to let the society around us convince us that our biblical goals are old-fashioned and naively idealistic. Rather, our visions are the true realism, the way God designed things to be, and we are bearers of the hope that God is at work to bring his design into existence.

Self-Disciplines and Couple Disciplines

We cannot, however, simply sit back and expect God to pull off the perfect marriage. We all know that marriage takes work, that it isn't always happy or fun, that it requires discipline and effort.

My favorite story about discipline concerns Yehudi Menuhin, the great concert violinist and conductor. When an awed listener praised his exquisite performance by insisting, "I would give my life to play like that," he gently replied, "I have."

We begin our reflections with that story because it demonstrates a critical truth that has been lost in our culture — that disciplines (such as the disciplines of practicing a violin or building a marriage) produce freedom and delight. People in our society perceive discipline only as an onerous burden and tiresome duty and fail to understand how it enables us truly to live and give our best.

Anyone who exercises regularly knows that daily workouts promote better circulation and breathing, more effective heartbeats, more firmly toned and stronger muscles, healthier bones, and even brighter emotions and clearer thinking. Those of us with debilitations know how daily workouts can prevent strokes, heart attacks, broken or crippled bones, amputations, and other complications or illnesses. How can anyone choose not to exercise?

How can anyone choose not to work at a marriage? (That is why we looked at the importance of goals first.) What personal and mutual disciplines are needed to strengthen marriages? There are already dozens of excellent books on improving marriage, so there is no need to attempt to imitate them here. Instead, let us simply reflect on ways in which our focus on an ethics of character and on the Christian community as the locus for nurturing virtues gives us extra insights into the process.

Children in our churches will be taught the importance of personal and mutual disciplines and virtues if they see them modeled in the adults of their communities. For example, youth have noticed — and commented on — the way Myron not only opens my car door but also hands me the seat belt. They see how much I enjoy praising Myron and talking about his gardening and other gifts and skills. They recognize that Myron's kindness in our marriage is a practiced habit, a developed virtue. As a mutual discipline, we speak only positively about each other in public (although that is so easy to do when it concerns Myron that it hardly seems a discipline!).

How can communities model for, and develop in, youth the disciplines of respect, habits of courtesy, and deeds of kindness that build marriage? How can my serving as a table parent on Wednesday nights help to form in the young people who sit there attitudes and actions that will gift future marriages? Myron doesn't just act kindly toward me — he is a kind person because of many nurturing influences. Our marriage is strong because he is good.

Myron's character serves as a model, not only to youth, but also to members of all ages in our congregation. Frequently people comment to me how inspiring it is to them to watch the way he takes care of me. (Of course, he isn't perfect. Myron always insists that I should report to my audiences and readers some of his bad attributes. I don't see any reason to, other than to demonstrate that he is humanly imperfect, so I'll simply tell you that he is.)

All of us in the Christian community are possible agents for positive teaching of virtues and nurturing of godly character. How can our congregations make better use of the marriage models that are available in our midst in order to strengthen other marriages and foster disciplines? How could we in the Church learn to be more confident in offering our models of relationships within God's design? Our marriages don't have to be spectacular or extraordinary. (We see from the struggles of the royal family in England that spectacular marriages carry burdens that are almost impossible to bear!) All they need to be is human — including the struggles, but most of all including the forgiveness that enables us to keep working on the marriage.

Probably the most important discipline for Christian marriage is that of mutual confession and absolution. So many marriages are ruined by accumulated grievances, well-watered resentments, heightened grudges. How much better if we "do not let the sun go down on [our] anger" (Eph. 4:26), but instead make it a constant practice to confess our faults and forgive each other's errors before the day's end.

In a society that hides and deceives, builds animosities and wreaks vengeance, the discipline of mutual repentance and forgiveness must be taught explicitly. How can we teach it to our children, practice it in worship settings in the congregation, develop the habit in all our relationships, model it as the essential ingredient in marriage? Again, a major factor in learning the practice is the way in which we envision the forgiveness of God. How thoroughly we know ourselves to be both desperately in need of forgiveness and yet totally forgiven no doubt influences our ability to forgive our spouses.

Various other disciplines for marriage come out of the fact that we are created and called to image God. For example, a God willing to sacrifice his own Son for the salvation of his people invites us to be willing to sacrifice our own interests for the well-being of a spouse. Again, the goals of our marriages in Christ challenge us to be open and honest with each other even as God is totally truthful with us. What other characteristics of God are especially valuable for building a sound marriage?

How can the Christian community also better practice and model the discipline of mutual submission? As members of the Body we know that God has brought us together for his purposes, and this is an especially important awareness in marriage. Because we believe that someday God will bring his plans for his people to completion, we can now rejoice in the ways in which we encourage and rebuke and question each other as aspects of, and participation in, God's polishing and perfecting work. Are we willing in the parish to give up our pride or position to submit to another for the well-being of the community and our witness to the surrounding culture? Are we willing to forego "winning" a marriage argument for the sake of God's purposes in the world?

A final discipline that is essential to the strength of both the Christian community and marriage and that is therefore an important dimension for our discussion is the fact that we nurture faithfulness by consciously upbuilding each other. If our congregations foster intentional and positive affirmation of each member, this will teach couples and children who bring these skills into friendships and future marriages how to nurture each other well.

Myron's fiftieth birthday this year gave those of us who love him a wonderful opportunity to encourage and affirm him. Many of his friends came to a surprise party at which gag gifts and jokes about age were forbidden. Instead, guests wrote out and read for the assembled group reasons why they appreciate Myron and stories of their happy memories of him. Then we put those papers in a scrapbook, to which we will add pictures of the party. The delight of that evening made us all realize how much more we could affirm each other — and how full is the happiness when we do so.

The Grace of God

The most important ingredient in Christian marriage is the grace of God. Grace brings us together and holds us together. The more we are aware of the giftedness of it all, the more thoroughly we can delight in it.

But we Christians are not very good at living under grace. Instead, we put ourselves under "performance principles,"[1] both in our relationship with God and with each other, and as a result we lose the possibility for living out of freedom and response rather than necessity and obligation. How can our times of worship and Bible study, our fellowship and service in the Church better enfold us in grace? How can we learn in marriage to be more frequent agents of grace for each other?

One essential habit in our marriage builds its gracefulness. When something goes wrong or the other person does something wrong, we both try to be quick to say, "I love you." Myron's constant love is pure grace — a gift I can't earn or deserve or repay, an incarnation of God's grace — and his assurance of its permanence frees me to confess my fault or to hope in spite of a new physical setback.

Another habit that enfolds us in grace is the farewell prayer at the end of our Sabbath day together. In this Havdalah we thank God especially for all the gifts of the special day, especially the gift of each other. This happens in other prayers, too — frequently at mealtimes — but Sabbath prayers particularly build the sense of grace in our marriage because one of the major purposes for celebrating the day is to become more aware of the grace of God.

One aspect of grace as the core of our union that never occurred to me until my devotional time this morning is that Christian marriage has a different perspective on suffering. In a world that tries to avoid pain, that denies the goodness or power of God because of the existence of evil, we who know that God is gracious recognize that suffering can also be a gift to us. Probably all of us can identify with the recognition that "the good old days" were usually not times of wealth and ease but times of struggle and hardship. Our tough times bring us together.

Many who question how it can be true that both God

1. This insightful phrase comes from Robin Scroggs's exposition of Romans in *Paul for a New Day* (Philadelphia: Fortress Press, 1977).

and evil exist and that God is both all-powerful and all-good operate from the assumption that the most important thing in life is to be happy. We who trust the grace of God know that it is more important to know the truth and to live for the good of all and not just self. I usually distinguish these two opposing opinions by differentiating between happiness and Joy.

What a great preserver of marriage it is to know that even when our life together is not "happy," especially because of outward circumstances that are inflicted upon us, we can still experience the Joy of knowing that God is good and that these evils which befall us can indeed work together for our good. The basis is grace, manifested undoubtedly for us in the cross of Jesus Christ and affirmed by the testimony of God's people throughout the history of the believing community. How can the Church declare this grace more thoroughly so that marriages can be nourished by it to be sustained in difficult times? In contrast to theologies that only falsely palliate and soothe, how can our Christian communities develop a more thorough understanding of suffering and a more effective ministry of care for those who are caught in suffering?[2]

How can we help couples not to be afraid of suffering, but to let it draw them closer together? Since all sorts of things can hurt our bodies, but nothing can hurt our souls unless we let it, we need to find ways to fortify God's people so that they can respond to suffering with hope and trust. Whether couples respond to their struggles with bitterness or allow those trials to bring about character growth depends on the perspectives with which they view suffering. What kinds of ministry can our Christian communities

2. Of the many books I have read on the subject of suffering, one of the best is Peter J. Kreeft's *Making Sense Out of Suffering* (Ann Arbor: Servant Books, 1986). See also Stanley Hauerwas, *Naming the Silences: God, Medicine, and the Problem of Suffering* (Grand Rapids: William B. Eerdmans, 1990).

offer to develop a perspective that grounds our hope in the belief that God is indeed both sovereign and good, able to care for us in our afflictions and wanting only the best for us when he allows times of affliction to come.[3]

The Beautiful Sign of Permanent Commitment

As has been stressed repeatedly in this book, my comments are meant to be discussion starters, places to begin to think about what the Christian community can become as the agent of God's gracious instruction concerning sexuality. Thus, my paragraphs about marriage are not intended to be a complete guide to solving problems or building perfect unions (though I will be overjoyed if they contribute a wee bit to that end). I am most interested in building the Church to be the Church, to pass on the narratives of the faith so that its members can learn God's design for their sexuality, and to foster the development of the necessary virtues so that this design can be chosen and enjoyed in deep friendships, strong marriages, and chaste sexuality.

That purpose makes me realize that what God's people know about sexual intercourse stands in great contrast to the attitude of the world that as long as nobody else is hurt it doesn't matter what one does. To think in such a way about such a holy act is to misunderstand its meaning entirely.

As we have previously noted, sexual intercourse is the special sign of a permanent and faithful commitment. Even to talk about it flippantly as "sex" as our society does is to

3. See my reflections on how the handicapped can better teach the Church how to respond to evil in *Joy in Our Suffering: The Book of Revelation and a Theology of Weakness* (St. Louis: Concordia Publishing House, 1993).

despoil it. (Perhaps you have noticed that throughout this book I have put that word in quotation marks. Maybe we could teach our churches' youth, when they are urged to "have sex," to answer, "I already have sex — I'm a fe/male.") Our language builds attitudes, habits that are an essential part of our character. If we speak of the act of union with respect, we are more likely to treat it with respect.

We will want in our Christian marriages to talk openly about our sexual union as a sign of God's faithfulness and to cherish it as such a sign. This gives us the freedom to work at pleasuring the other and to enjoy the possibilities of our conjugal love even as God delights to gift us. Again, the discipline creates the freedom. Having withheld from sexual intercourse throughout friendship and courtship gives great delight to a couple on their wedding night and thereafter when at last the gift is theirs to share.

Our emphasis on sexual union as a "sign" also takes the pressure off intercourse to preserve the marriage. A theology of "Sign" is vastly needed in our churches for more reasons than marriage. Many Christian denominations overemphasize signs instead of focusing on what they point to.

If you were heading for a retreat and saw a sign that gave directions to the camp, you certainly wouldn't park your car at the sign. Though the sign is a reality in itself and a good reality at that, it certainly is not what we ultimately want — namely, the entity to which it points.

Similarly, miracles are called "signs" in the Gospel of John (and there are only the perfect seven of them to emphasize that they are representatives) to underscore that they are not the ultimate reality which John is trying to manifest. The signs are wonderful in themselves, but they are really valuable because they point to the divinity of Christ. We shouldn't park our faith at the signs; rather, we should let the miracles of healing or whatever point us to who Christ really is and his centrality for faith.

123

In the same way, the sign of sexual union is a wonderful reality in itself, but its ultimate meaning lies outside of its immediate pleasure. It is a sign, a gift to be enjoyed and to be grateful for, but not in any way where we should park our marriage car (and certainly not where we should park our car outside of marriage). When sexual expression is not under pressure to be the be-all and end-all of marriage, it can be more thoroughly enjoyed and explored. It takes its proper place as the fullest, most precious expression of a unique commitment, a covenant promise to share the rest of life in order to manifest the grace and faithfulness of God to the world.

11 *Divorce*

Many of us grew up in churches which taught (mostly implicitly) that divorce is the worst sin on the face of the globe and that those who are divorced should be avoided in order not to catch the plague. How terrible that God's gracious warnings have been turned into condemnations of those who suffer the great tragedy of broken oneness. For many of us, experiences of rejection, betrayal, and abandonment enabled us to see the critical need for bringing grace to any discussion about the issues of divorce.

On the other hand, bringing grace back dare not mean making it flabby. In total rejection of churches' former condemnations, the pendulum often swings too far in the opposite direction and accommodates too readily our culture's easy divorce. In the middle of these extremes, the Church could recognize that divorce is a great tragedy and sometimes necessary (as Jesus said, because of adultery), but it is certainly to be avoided if at all possible by supporting marriages as couples try to work things out.

As we can see in these pendulum swings, divorce is one of myriads of issues that get confused if we are not able to make precise nuances. This is not to be nit-picky about words; rather, it is to make as clear as possible the questions that must be asked. For example, we can avoid extremes by saying that divorce is usually not so much a sin as it is the result of sin and brokenness. Often it is not so much the breaking of the marriage bond as it is the decisive declaration that the marriage has already been irretrievably broken, not by such merely flippant categories of disruption as "incompatibility," but by adulterous bonding with another person. Sometimes in our violent world, divorce, though certainly not God's best, is critically necessary for preservation of life.

The rate of divorce has reached such astronomical heights in our culture because of the great emphasis that is placed on emotional satisfaction in the family. This is partly a result of the sexual idolatry of our times, and it is partly caused by the pressures inherent in the type of society we have. We saw in Part I how a technological society both causes a greater need for finding comfort in the home and also prohibits such comfort because family members bring back the psychological strains of life outside the home and because they have been prevented from developing the requisite skills for creating and expressing intimacy by the pace and toys/tools of the milieu.

The biblical picture is intense. God does not say he hates the person who is divorced, but he does say, "I hate divorce" (Mal. 2:16). It violates his design for marriage to be permanent, so he warns and rebukes the children of Israel; but he does not disown the persons involved, as churches often do. To imitate God in this matter would be also to hate divorce, to see it as the rupture of God's plan that it is, and then to do everything we can to prevent it and to bring healing to those who have been broken by it. Since many of the pieces necessary for this chapter have already been suggested in previous sections, we will bring them together here into a more cohesive whole to formulate necessary questions for the Church.

Preventive Medicine

In literature, a tragedy occurs because a character flaw — such as pride or jealousy — in the protagonist inexorably leads to his or her downfall. If divorce is a tragedy, we recognize that changes of character are necessary to avoid it. How can the Christian community build in its youth the necessary virtues and attitudes and the best understanding of God's design for lifelong marriage so that they have a good chance in the future of enjoying a marriage that lasts? A major key is teaching explicitly that divorce is not an option in Christian marriage, but this declaration must be nuanced carefully to avoid condemnation of the divorced and to provide consolation for broken families.

One of my husband's friends told him many years ago that she remembered saying to herself even on her wedding day that if the marriage didn't work out she could always get a divorce. With such an attitude, she admitted, it was much easier to give up on the marriage. How can our communities recover the "old-fashioned" biblical notion that divorce is impossible in a Christian marriage, but without the condemnation this foundation formerly included?

Obviously we see the significance of our foundations for character formation in this matter. Those whose characters are founded upon the overarching value of permanent commitment will follow through with virtues of patience, endurance, perseverance, and reconciling love that will continue to seek means for working out difficult problems in a marriage. If a person's character is subject to giving up when the going gets hard, that person is much more likely to end a marriage without attempting to solve its problems.

How can the Church make more available for young people to see, in contrast to our faithless society, the perseverance required to stay committed? How can we point to the virtues of steadfastness when we talk about both God and his people? In the previous chapter we discussed finding ways to celebrate long-standing marriages; we can also ask about finding ways to celebrate other manifestations of patience and commitment, of love that overcomes its opposition.

An additional part of our preventive medicine will be to build in our young people an understanding of marriage as outlined in Part II and in the previous chapter. It is especially important to help them learn, in contradiction to what they hear in our culture, that it is not true that "sex" is the most important thing in a relationship — a fallacy that sets marriages up to fail when the excitement wanes. In our next chapter we will consider questions about how to nurture such a vision in children.

Another major aspect of preventive medicine is for the community to give young people better counsel when they are in the process of making decisions about marriage. What kind of communities do we need to be so that youth will turn to respected adults and seek the counsel of godly members of the Body when they are contemplating marriage? Are there any specific structures or procedures that we could establish in our congregations so that it would be easier for youth to gain that necessary counsel in a non-intimidating way?

Once an engagement is announced, what kind of pre-marital counseling do we offer?[1] One congregation in Oregon matches prospective couples with partners from a long-standing marriage. The bride-to-be meets frequently with the wife, who takes her under her wing to display the virtues and attitudes helpful through the years, and the husband does the same for the groom-to-be.

Even the wedding ceremony makes a big difference. Do our churches hold marriage ceremonies that fall into the patterns of the society around us — focusing on extrav-

1. One good resource might be Joyce Huggett's *Growing into Love: Before You Marry* (Downers Grove, IL: InterVarsity Press, 1982).

agant expense and show and forgetting that God is the center of this union that is now beginning? What kinds of alternative wedding services can we plan so that the purposes of Christian marriage are highlighted?[2]

After the Wedding

After the marriage ceremony a couple needs the Christian community to give them full support in maintaining the marriage and resisting the cultural current toward easy divorce. In the previous chapter we suggested some ways in which congregations can offer such support.

If minor troubles develop in a couple's relationship, do our congregations provide opportunities for help? For example, do our parishes sponsor small-group Bible studies in which couples can be supported by other group members in the needs and struggles of their marriage? Do teams of elders and deacons genuinely function as troubleshooters to offer counsel and listening ears?

If major troubles erupt in a marriage, how can the community enfold the parties involved to give them support and to help them work things through? A pastor once reported to me how his congregation surrounded a couple who had been torn apart by the husband's affair. Men of the parish told their brother how much they loved him and therefore how much it pained them to see him destroy his family and the family of his mistress. Their powerful love wooed him to repentance, gave him the courage to break off the affair, and supported him as he went through a long process of reconciliation with his wife. Simultaneously, women of the congregation enfolded their sister and en-

2. If you are interested in a copy of the alternative service we wrote for our wedding, contact me at 304 Fredericksburg Way, Vancouver, WA 98664-2147.

couraged her to pour out her pain. Their enormous love brought some healing for the stabs of rejection and betrayal and gave her the courage to forgive her husband and begin the process of rebuilding the marriage. Today that marriage is strong and healthy — much more so than before the affair because of the power of forgiveness at work.

Do we believe that the grace of God is strong enough to heal even the deep wounds of adultery? Why don't we more often take the bold steps necessary to save a marriage that is on the brink of disaster? What can we do to strengthen the vision in our parishes that love can overcome all such evil? How can we more thoroughly teach the vision of Hosea and Gomer — the love that welcomes back the wayward one, the love that intensely and patiently yearns for reconciliation and restoration?

It is especially important that we teach in the Church our common responsibility to do everything possible to seek reconciliation. As the Psalmist and Peter say, we are called to "seek peace and pursue it" (Ps. 34:14; 1 Pet. 3:11), to do whatever is available to us. Thus, in broken relationships we will try and try again and then try once more, but we will also be comforted by the assurance that we are set free from the burden if our efforts continue to fail because the other party is not willing to be reconciled. Often this happens in cases of adultery; the one guilty of adultery continues to obstruct attempts at reconciliation because of unwillingness to give up the affair. Then the person more innocent (for never in our sinfulness is anyone totally innocent) can be comforted by the fact that her or his efforts were faithful responses to God's design.

After the Divorce

If the tragedy of a divorce is unavoidable — perhaps because of adultery or severe alcoholism or various forms of noncooperation in the reconciliation process — then we who are God's people have a whole new set of responsibilities for our brothers and sisters. Most especially, how can we offer comfort to the one who tried and was not successful? That is the time when the one who has been rejected needs more than anything to be assured that he or she is a worthwhile person, and yet, sadly, that is often the time when other members of the parish avoid him or her because they "don't know what to say." (We must, above all, be sure to say that the person is loved by all of us in the community — and, more so, by God.)

After abandonment and betrayal, the victims need hugs, listening ears, company, time to themselves without the responsibilities of children, the assurance that they have done their best to mend the tear, and a great deal of patience. What plans can the community make so that those who are suffering receive the thorough support they need? This is especially important because of the distinction we made in Part I between genital and social sexuality. Often those who have been abandoned by a spouse become involved in sexual affairs because there is not enough social support and affirmation to keep them from desperately seeking comfort in genital sexual expression.

Conversely, Matthew 18:15-20 gives us a plan for confronting the spouse who refuses reconciliation, but we must always remember that this plan is surrounded by parables of forgiveness. Our ultimate goal in dealing with a wayward one is always restoration. If persons reject the efforts of an individual, of a small group, and of the entire Body, then we will treat them as a "Gentile or tax collector" — that is, as outsiders whom we want to invite into belief and acceptance of the values of the community. How can we prevent the community from giving up on such persons? Does our love imitate God's in his never-ending search for the lost one?

Perhaps our responsibility after a divorce will be to

console someone who failed miserably and is filled with regret. In what ways will we both declare and incarnate forgiveness? How can we help the person to have the courage to start again, to get past the overwhelming guilt and regret that immobilizes?

We all recognize that divorce severely wounds the children involved. They blame themselves for their parents' unresolvable conflicts; they don't know how to relate to double sets of parents; they develop bad habits of manipulation and deception to find balm for their pain. In what ways can other members of the community be friends, systems of support, perhaps alternate parents for them? Which men in the congregation could be friends with their mother so that they can see models of gracious and caring males, father figures, positive images of God? Which women of the congregation could provide the mothering nurture that is necessary for them to thrive? Abandoned women and the children of divorce are often the most needy "widows and orphans" in our culture, and God's people are called to care for them. For example, what can we do to help augment their (usually) greatly reduced financial resources?

Many divorced women have talked with me about how to help their children recognize that divorce is not God's best. In the Church we need to learn better how to speak out of brokenness, to acknowledge our failures in ways that invite others to choose otherwise. This is an especially important place for other members of the community to assist single parents, to help them nurture their children with a vision of lasting marriage, with the hope that the mistakes of a child's parents need not be repeated in his or her life.

Second Marriages

Once again we must make careful nuances. On the one hand, we do not want to soften the biblical prohibition against divorce as a rending of a permanent union. On the other hand, we recognize that for many a second marriage might be one of God's best gifts to bring healing and grace after the ravages of divorce.

One key question, therefore, must be whether the individual and we, the community, have done all we can to restore the first marriage. Has a second marriage on the part of the former spouse made reconciliation impossible? It is important for the Christian community to recognize our responsibility in the process of trying to heal a rift, for rarely can the one abandoned bring a spouse to repentance.

Other questions are raised by the difficulties inherent in caring for blended families. That God's design for permanent marriage works better is displayed by the stickiness of arrangements for children of various marriages to spend time with their double sets of parents. Yet a second marriage is a frequent reality — and can be a genuine source of healing for the children — and so it calls the community of God's people to new tasks in the need to support families who struggle with all the problems of bringing together two families (or three if there are children in the new union).

Could the work of the congregation sometimes be to warn parents who are considering remarriage of the dangers of trying to blend families and to support them as friends instead? Could we provide special outlets for the children — perhaps a trusted adult to whom they can vent their rage and feelings of abandonment? What other means might we offer to enable new family structures to be permanent?

Probably you join me in feeling at the end of this chapter that the needs are enormous — because the pain of divorce is so great and the tide of easy divorce in our culture is almost too overwhelming to counteract. That is why we need the whole community to help in the supportive and healing processes. Because God's instructions for sexual faithfulness are true to who we are in his design, we seek to follow them as well as we can. However, we also know that his grace and forgiveness, incarnated in the community, are large enough to bring healing for all of us who suffer in the brokenness of our personal sinfulness and the idolatries of our world.

12 *Nurturing Children*

In the midst of my mulling over the organization of the various facets of this chapter, I was struck forcibly by the thought of how radical a shift occurred in people's thinking, not only about genital sexual relationships, but also about children, when human beings learned how to control whether children were born. Before conception could be prevented by other than natural means, children were received; now the couple (or even single individuals) decides whether or not to have them. This paradigmatic shift turns the focus away from the former emphasis on the children to a new stress on the choice of the parents.

This shift in perspective is enormously significant. It changes the major question from "How shall we raise children?" to "Do I want children?" or even "How can I avoid having children and still enjoy sexual pleasure?"

Why Do We Have Children?

If our fundamental question concerns our own choices about whether or not to have children, this signals a basic

135

difference in character that must certainly affect the way we raise children. The focus will be on how the children can give value to us, on what they contribute to our lives. Some might choose to have children because they will carry on the family name, might accomplish what the parents could not, will be fun to have around, or can provide for the parents in their old age.

On the other hand, some people in our society choose not to have children for a variety of terribly selfish reasons — they are too expensive, they would hamper one's life-style too much, the world is so dangerous that it would be too much trouble to raise them in it. Of course, there are also some good reasons for not having children, such as limited health — my quarrel is not with those.

The point to note is the selfishness demonstrated by many of the reasons for positive or negative choices about producing and caring for children. In an ethics of character, our primary question always is "What kind of people are we or are we becoming?" If a couple's reason for having children comes from a fundamentally self-centered concern for their own gain, with what kind of character will they nurture their children?

The Christian community offers a quite astonishing alternative to the world in this matter. We admit that having children IS a great burden, but it is one we gladly choose for the sake of the Kingdom of God. Moreover, whether or not a couple has children may depend upon their role in the community. Some Christians might be childless for the same reason that others are single — in order to dedicate their lives more fully to the spiritual care of others.

In a chapter entitled "The Moral Value of the Family," Stanley Hauerwas reminds us that in former societies the main role of the family was to reproduce and to rear children for the future. He laments the fact that the prevailing cultural assumptions of today's society leave parents bereft

136

of any notion that being a parent is an office of the community and not a willful act. To them belongs the primary (but not sole) responsibility for passing on the values of God's people. Their key role enables them to ask children to behave in certain ways, to live as the Christian community lives, to believe as we believe.[1]

Several aspects of an ethics of character are involved in the recognition of this role. We realize that, as an alternative society, we who are members of the Christian community have behaviors, life-styles, and beliefs worth passing on — that what we proclaim is the truth and worthy of acceptance. Moreover, in spite of the state of our world, we declare by bringing children into the world that there is hope, that God is indeed sovereign and good, and that he is able to use us as agents in his care for all his children.

Nurturing Children for Sexual Character

Our purpose in this section is certainly not to offer simplistic solutions for all parenting problems. As with all of the other subjects touched upon here, there are all kinds of excellent books of instructions for gaining the requisite parenting skills. Our specific concern for the sexual character of persons, however, raises important questions to guide our nurturing processes.

Most fundamental, if we want our children's understanding of their sexuality to be different from that of the world around them (as previously sketched), then we cannot suddenly begin to teach them when they are teenagers

1. Hauerwas, *A Community of Character* (Notre Dame: University of Notre Dame Press, 1981), pp. 159 and 173. See especially his chapters 8 and 9, "The Moral Value of the Family" and "The Family: Theological Reflections," pp. 155-74.

about holding alternative values. It is important that we begin when they are tiny to invite them into the delight of being different. We teach them that they are special — not, as public school "self-esteem" programs commonly do, by encouraging them to look inward, but by enfolding them constantly in God's grace and forgiveness, the divine design and salvation, which set us free to follow Jesus in pursuing the Kingdom of God.

How can we instruct our children in the values of that Kingdom without falling off into either of two extremes — on the one hand, the provincialism that would pull us away from the surrounding culture into our own separate enclave, or, on the other hand, the enculturation that cannot distinguish between our values and those of the society when they must disagree? It is the long-standing question of how to be in the world without being of it.

In Chapter 5, I sketched some of the differences in my childhood because our family's life was directed outside itself. In this chapter my goal is that we recognize that all aspects of a child's life are part of the difference — that, like the earliest Christians, we are indeed strangers and sojourners here and choose noticeable alternatives for the way we live.

Take, for example, the celebration of holidays like Christmas or Easter. What can we do to help our children to learn that we have different understandings about those holy days and also to help them enjoy being different in our celebration of them? My parents followed many old German Lutheran customs to make the days different for us so that we both knew what the celebration was all about and didn't feel deprived not to have all the material accoutrements other children had. Advent wreaths with candles for every day of the season lit our nightly Advent devotions with hymns sung in harmony; worship was emphasized as the primary activity of the entire month (with Advent services every week and several special services on Christmas Eve and Christmas Day). Instead of Santa Claus, we focused on the Christ Child coming to our home.

When doing workshops on alternative Christmas celebrations, I am often asked, "What's wrong with Santa Claus?" Basically what is wrong with Santa Claus as he is portrayed today is that the theology is backwards. Santa Claus teaches children that if they are good, then they will be rewarded. The Christ Child comes instead to tell us that, even though we cannot be good, God gives us the greatest gift of all anyway.

This simple illustration of a seasonal celebration demonstrates the process that parents can practice with other issues of family life. It is possible to talk about Santa Claus in a Christian way, emphasizing the goodness and social concern of the original St. Nicholas and how he exemplified the gifting of God. The crucial point is that we help our children to know that what we believe — namely, that salvation is not only an enormously wonderful and totally essential gift but also that it is the entire reason for the season — influences the way we celebrate.

Similarly, what we believe affects how we spend our money, what we wear, how we allocate our time, whether we watch this violent or immoral television program, what we do with our Sundays, how we relate to our neighbors, for whom and what we vote, what occupations we choose, and how we behave sexually.

What kind of special activities could we engage in to build in our children the mind-set that we make careful decisions as Christians so that our behaviors and attitudes follow the way of Jesus? Can we prevent their whining that we should buy them something in stores because they already have learned that we choose carefully how to spend our money so that we have more to give away to those in need? Perhaps we can take them to a Habitat for Humanity building project or to a medical clinic or tutoring service for the poor so that they can participate in sharing our wealth with those who are less fortunate. We can invite our children to help make good choices in the grocery shopping or to assist us when we deliver food to a shelter. Perhaps we can save up particular treats to make the Sabbath special — to teach our children that we cannot truly enjoy feasting if we never fast and that pleasures are more delightful and meaningful if we forego them at times.

These ideas are especially important for training our children in a biblical understanding of their sexuality, for the great delight of sexual union is magnified much more profoundly when it has been saved for one and only one relationship. Our gluttonous society will never understand that pleasure is heightened when it is reserved, so we must explicitly proclaim that fact and incarnate it in our own habits if we want our children to delight in God's design for sexual intercourse only within its proper framework of marriage.

One of the keys to raising our children in an alternative way is conversation. Probably you have seen the statistics frequently proffered by sociologists of the extremely small amount of quality time spent by parents in our society with their children. In the Christian community we want to be decisively different. One of the major reasons why the Church of Jesus Christ of Latter-day Saints is growing like crazy is its emphasis on family life. Many of the converts to Mormonism are drawn to its insistence on a weekly, intimate family evening composed of Scripture reading, special activities, and discussions.

Can our families institute such a special night? For those who are just starting their families, it is important to do so when the children are first born so that the habit is established before they get involved in so many school activities. In contrast to our society's "passing in the night" living arrangements, can our families specifically set aside time for devotions, meals together, and intimate conversations, so that when the children start wondering about their sexuality the patterns of discussion are already set? My former secretary built wonderful relationships with her three children by "tucking them in" every night, even when they were in high school, so that there was always a special time to talk.

Because this book's ultimate goal in giving these illustrations of an alternative life-style is to build in our children preventive medicine for their sexual behavior, the most important activities that must be deliberately addressed are their listening to music and viewing of television programs and movies. How can we teach our children to discriminate — first of all, to choose carefully what they watch and listen to, and second, to cast out values that contradict God's designs? Because the media in our culture so explicitly promote sexual values with which we disagree, we must be more intentional in avoiding them, discounting them, contradicting them, and, most important, demonstrating that God's values are more satisfying, more truthful to who we are.

I don't have children and I don't have a television set, so I know that many readers might cast off what I write as hopelessly idealistic, but the importance of supervising media consumption remains. Would we serve our children garbage for dinner? Of course not. But if we would not feed their bodies with toxic materials, why on earth do we feed their souls with trash? I cannot imagine letting a small child watch television without my supervision and, as often as possible, my companionship.

I used to speak very mildly about the dangers of television — until I read the book *Endangered Minds* and learned more scientifically what harm it causes, and until I started doing workshops with teenagers and saw how profoundly it affects their sexual attitudes. Now I'm on a campaign to weed out its polluting effects on our lives, but since there are many other such campaigns I don't need to dwell on the issue here. My theme in this book is intentionality. If we want to raise children for godly sexual behavior, then we must be intentional in forming understandings and attitudes when they are young, so that they have the strength of character to choose such behavior when they are older. We must deliberately reject the bombardment of the media's immorality, the sexual looseness in fashion, the glib way in which people talk about "sex."

Many Christian parents are upset about the distribution of condoms in high schools or the "sex education" programs in elementary schools. Perhaps these should be specifically fought — depending upon the local situation and the types of programs. Much more important, however, is how we have prepared our children BEFORE they encounter such things. What kind of moral education are we doing in the home and in our churches to teach children the biblical understanding of their sexuality? How are we preparing them to resist the ideas of secular society and to choose behavior that flows from what they believe?

You might by now be feeling overwhelmed by all of this and thinking that the task of Christian parenting is too hard, even impossible in this society. Two aspects of our call as parents need to be underscored to give us hope.

First of all, in light of many passages in the Bible, we can realize that in our many tasks as parents we do the best we can to image God. The picture in Genesis 1 of our roles to image God as male and female and the Ephesians 6:4 instructions to bring our children up in the "nurture and admonition of the Lord — not provoking them to anger" put all that we have said above into perspective. We are not expected to be God for our children, but to do whatever we can in God's stead. How can we learn better to put ourselves under the same grace in which we want to nurture our children?

Of course, fathers and mothers are fallible human beings. None of us could ever parent as well as we would like to. But we can humbly admit to our children that we are doing the best we can to serve as representatives of God's fathering and mothering. In our failings, our chil-

dren can always know that their totally successful Parent
is always there for them. Meanwhile, our methods of
parenting are guided and our courage for the task is
heightened by the way in which God reveals himself in his
care for us.

Second, parenting is not a duty to be borne alone.
Rather, it is also the responsibility of the whole Christian
community. This Sunday morning one of the boys from my
Wednesday evening dinner table group came to me after I
finished teaching adult Bible class to show me something
he had made. What a privilege it is to have a friendship
with this teenager! I hold it as a sacred duty (besides a
delight) to affirm him, to encourage him, to be a very small
part in forming him into a godly young man.

How can we better instruct our congregations so that
everyone in the entire group knows that he or she shares
in the responsibility for nurturing the children in our
midst? For example, we can remind members of the parish
of the vows they make when children are baptized to support them in their faith. We have previously discussed in
this book the importance of holding up the social sexuality
of all of our youth so that they do not feel desperate for
intimacy and seek it in genital sexual fulfillment.

How open are our parishes to the presence and contributions of children? Do we give them opportunities to
serve in important ways as a valuable part of the community? In one congregation in upstate New York the younger
elementary school children lead the chanting of the Introit
every Sunday. They recognize that this is their job — and
a very important one at that — and they are eager to play
their bells and teach the congregation how to sing the
Psalm for the day. This not only teaches them a lot of
worship skills, but it also and especially deepens their faith
in God and their self-esteem, both essential building blocks
for the kind of character that can resist the sexual tides of
our society.

How can our parishes more thoroughly surround families to provide community support and the input of extra adults who care for raising children with the values of the Bible? Everyone knows that it is easier to stick to certain rules and regulations in dealing with one's children if other parents choose the same guidelines. It is also far easier for children to choose positive values if those values are attractively incarnated in the adults of the Church.

This emphasis on community works in two ways. Not only does the community help to nurture children, but also the children learn that they, too, have responsibilities in and to the community. They are part of its modeling; they, too, demonstrate to the world the delight of choosing God's alternative. How can we help our youth recognize that they serve a great need in the world by resisting society's looseness about "sex" and by demonstrating instead the goodness of a deliberate choice to wait for sexual union till marriage?

The prevailing assumption in our culture is that children should be allowed to make their own "intelligent choices" — about religion, about their sexuality. In contrast, as Stanley Hauerwas reminds us, in the Christian community we will want to raise our children to be worthy of carrying on the traditions of their ancestors.[2] Thus, an important task of the community is to celebrate its values and invite children to participate in the delight of choosing to be faithful to those values as a gift to the world — and to themselves!

Bearing Children and Sexual Union

In the Christian community we want to reconnect the link, which has been torn apart by the proliferation of contraceptive methods, between sexual intercourse and repro-

2. Hauerwas, *A Community of Character*, p. 169.

duction. I am not saying that contraceptive methods are wrong (though I am opposed to those, such as the IUD, which abort an already fertilized egg). Rather, I am urging Christians to consider (with the community's help) whether God has called us to be parents or not. The vision for nurturing children in faith and faithful life is valuable both after and before marriage — to help us know what to do when the children have arrived and to keep us from ripping sexual union out of its context in the larger responsibility of providing a permanent marriage for the care of children.

One indication of the selfishness inherent in the modern shift in fundamental questions is the phenomenal neglect of children in many contemporary books on "sex." How can it be so easily forgotten that a natural — no, we should say *God-given* — result and purpose of sexual intercourse is the conception of a child. To ask questions about that integral connection will display for our children the consequences of their sexual behavior. In Christian families we want to raise those issues, but not with the old-fashioned (before modern methods of contraception) approach that tried to keep kids out of "sex" by making them afraid of pregnancy. Rather, the Church would do well to formulate the questions again to reconnect our society's scramble for rights with the correlative responsibilities. We will see in the following chapter on abortion how critical it is to remind our world of these fundamental connections.

13 *Abortion*

We must define our interest here in the abortion issue very narrowly, for the arguments range widely and cover all kinds of related subjects, almost all of which lie outside the scope of this book. I wish we could even begin to pursue here such topics as asking better questions about the terms with which the issues are described — for example, what does it mean to be "pro-life" if we do nothing to clean up the ghetto in which a child might have to live?

One dimension of the abortion debates, however, does specifically lie within the domain of this book's focus. Whenever I hear arguments about abortion, I am astonished that a major question is never asked. Women repeatedly demand to have the right to choose what they want for their own bodies, but rarely does the media or any public figure ask in response, "Don't you also therefore have the responsibility to choose carefully what you do with your body before conceiving?"

Wendell Berry states this perspective best in a forum in *Harper's Magazine*. He reminds us that a pregnancy is not an isolated event. Pregnancy is connected to sexuality, sexuality is connected to fertility, fertility is connected to nature. In choosing to take part in sexuality, one chooses, wittingly or not, to take part in an enterprise far greater than oneself. If one is to be human, one must manage to be generous toward the results.[1]

Our society really has lost its foundations — as many more knowledgeable historians, sociologists, and ethicists have frequently commented. How can it be that in our mad pursuit of individual rights and happiness we have forgotten to ask about the accompanying responsibilities?[2] If a person has the right to practice medicine, then he also has the responsibility never to use that role to harm someone. If an individual earns the right to drive a car, then her license also calls her to the responsibility of driving carefully.

"The right to sexual pleasure demands the correlative responsibility to bear the consequences of that indulgence." I put that sentence in quotation marks because it is true and can be an argument with the rights-demanders in their own terms. However, I cringe to use such language, for it is also symptomatic of all that has been lost because our society has ripped sexual intercourse out of its framework in a permanent marriage open to welcoming children into the family.

1. Berry, "She's Come for an Abortion. What Do You Say?" *Harper's Magazine* 285, 1710 (Nov. 1992): 50.
2. This is rooted, of course, in the more fundamental problem that modern society has lost several basic foundations for thinking. These are wonderfully outlined by Peter J. Kreeft in chapter 10 of *Making Sense Out of Suffering* (Ann Arbor: Servant Books, 1986) as modernity's "New *Summum Bonum*," "Loss of Faith in Ultimate Meaning," and "Forgetfulness" of "Heaven and Hell," "Solidarity," "Original Sin," "Vicarious Atonement," and "Justice" (pp. 169-82).

How can we use rights language to talk about a relationship of total commitment that expresses itself in a holy act of physical union? We do not demand our "rights" from a spouse whom we love and cherish, with whom we are intimately joined not only physically but also, more importantly, in the Church's witness to the great faithfulness of God.

How can we ask about the right to control our own bodies when our bodies are the temples of God and are to be used for his purposes? Questions about a developing fetus are inherently connected to questions about the purposes of genital sexuality, but the latter do not seem to be asked in the debates.

Besides being related to the larger questions concerning sexuality, the abortion debates are also related to our recognition in the previous chapter that Christian marriage promotes raising children to carry on the faith. Stanley Hauerwas comments on the ways in which public liberalism has created an emphasis on the individual that destroys the values of "family." He cites as an example how abortion has become a matter of an individual's right to control her own body, rather than a matter of a family's understanding of the importance of welcoming children into the world.[3]

Hauerwas's question is superb because it does not let either side in the abortion debates off the hook. What are we doing in our society to make life more welcoming for children born into poverty? What is the Church doing to support pregnant teenagers so that they can personally be more welcoming? Are we creating jobs and changing the welfare system so that families can stay together and be more welcoming? Most important for this book, are we helping to change persons' ideas about their sexuality so that sexual pleasure can again be connected to the responsibility of welcoming children into the world?

3. Hauerwas, *A Community of Character* (Notre Dame: University of Notre Dame Press, 1981), pp. 158-60 and 196-229.

The problem of abortion in present society stems — not solely, but primarily — from the prior matter of the sexual idolatry of our times. To ask about the former requires deeper asking about the latter. If the Church is going to have an impact in questioning the morality of abortion, we must do a more thorough job of questioning the larger frameworks — the sexual morality that produces "unwanted" pregnancies, the violence and perversion that produce rape and incest, the selfishness that does not want to bear any responsibility.

14 *Teenagers, Dating, and "Sex"*

H ow shall the church talk with teenagers about their sexual lives?[1] Everywhere I go, I see and hear youth — both in and out of the Church — yearning for better alternatives, good models, biblical guidance, and hope.

As Stanley Hauerwas points out, the world around us deals with youth's sexuality in primarily two ways. One of these, cultural realism, says that it is too late to do anything about the sexual situation in our country. Present sexual behavior in our society is a fact that we might as well accept.

A second type of response is the romantic. The notion still flourishes that love is the necessary condition for "sex," though our culture has a loose definition of what such love actually entails.

Hauerwas reminds us, in contrast, that in the Church the question of "sex" before marriage is part of the larger

---

1. One especially good study guide for adults on this subject that stresses the forming of character in community is C. Ellis Nelson's *Helping Teenagers Grow Morally* (Louisville: Westminster/John Knox Press, 1989).

issue of what kind of persons we need to be in order to do the task the Christian community asks of us, whether we are single persons or married.[2] How much would be changed in Christian youths' basic thinking about this question if this integral connection with all that we are and do would be remembered.

Obviously, all of the previous chapters in this book are prerequisite to this one. Only when we recover the larger understanding of God's design for genital sexuality and families and the even larger understanding of what it means to be God's people in the world can we talk with teenagers about their sexuality in ways that can be really helpful for guiding them to better choices for their own lives. Ultimately, our goal is for our Christian youth to experience the Joy of following God's plan for chaste friendships and for sexual union only when it is a covenant sign of permanent commitment in marriage.

How wonderful it would be if the young people in our churches, instead of being swept up into the sexual immorality of their peers, could be leaders in offering their peers a better alternative — namely, God's design for human sexuality. Correlative to that would be the ability of Christian youth to build deep, nongenital friendships. In great contrast to our culture, which focuses on physical attractiveness and genital sexual expression and exploitation, the Church can be a place that nurtures multidimensioned relationships.

If we want to build such an understanding in our young people, how can we best lay down the foundations? As this book keeps emphasizing, that work begins long before the children start asking questions about their sex-

2. Hauerwas, *A Community of Character* (Notre Dame: University of Notre Dame Press, 1981), pp. 177-81 and 194. Especially helpful is the chapter entitled "Sex in Public: Toward a Christian Ethic of Sex," pp. 175-95.

uality. But if we are specifically talking with youth about the subject, we must start with all of the foundational ideas of this book. In my presentations for church youth or parents' groups about sexuality, I draw pictures. (Since I can't draw whatsoever, that's always good for laughs.) The first picture I draw is a simple triangle to illustrate how knowing our God as a Trinity undergirds this subject, as we outlined in Chapter 7.

Then a simple vertical line will help us sketch for young people the critical distinction, so confused by our society, between social and genital sexuality, as described in Chapter 2. The importance of thorough support for our social sexuality, emphasized in that same chapter, can be illustrated with a simple square, around which we label the various groups of people holding up our "trampolines." At this point, how can we make sure that the young people realize that we, the Christian community, are there for them? What can we do so that their "trampolines" do not fall down if they lack adequate family and friends to support their personal identities?

My picture of a typewriter, to illustrate the emphases in Chapter 3, always looks pretty funny, but it provides a way to talk about God's design and about how unfunny it is to violate that design to our own loss and grief. This picture is critical, for our society does not believe in ultimate purposes, in the transcendent design of God. Consequently, our world ignores the larger framework that is vitally necessary for any true understanding of human sexuality. How can we help our youth to recognize how destructive the modern rejection of the Absolute truly is?

Next in my presentation to teens about "sex" are two drawings that represent relationships. I tell them about the time in the midst of my graduate work in English when a dormmate eagerly told me she was moving out to live with her boyfriend. My response was to stammer out something like this: "Claudia, you'll probably think that I'm just awfully old-fashioned and terribly prudish, but I wish you wouldn't move in with your boyfriend. I'm afraid that a relationship built only on sex is too fragile, and it will tip over in time. Then you will be so hurt — and I care about you too much to want you to have to go through all that pain. Besides, you won't be able to trust anyone for a long time if this fellow drops you."

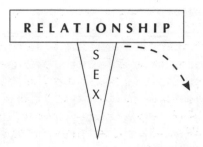

Claudia did think I was awfully prudish, and she moved out of the dorm. But two months later she was back and immediately came to see me. "You were right," she lamented. "When the sex got boring, he dumped me." Ever since then this question has nagged me: how could Christians be more effective at warning people of the emptiness and disappointment, the anger and destruction of trust, the resentment and frustration, or the grief and loss that will be suffered if we pull sexual intercourse out of its rightful context? Some of those feelings are bound to result because a "one-flesh" union has been created and then ripped apart. Part of a person's self is lost in the process. A relationship that is built merely on the single pillar of sexual attraction is much too unstable and is bound to fail and fall. The result is the tragic death of oneness — and whether the person is consciously aware of it or not, the emptiness of loss is there.

In contrast, I usually tell the kids about my friendship with Myron, drawing another pillar under the relationship

153

with each aspect of the story. When educators of youth tell such stories, it is especially important that we offer positive models of nongenital romance to help young people see (because they don't very often in contemporary media) that loving relationships are even more tender and beautiful when they are not exploitative or lustful, when they don't pluck sexual union from its rightful place of protection.

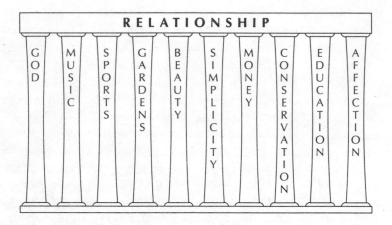

RELATIONSHIP

GOD · MUSIC · SPORTS · GARDENS · BEAUTY · SIMPLICITY · MONEY · CONSERVATION · EDUCATION · AFFECTION

I tell the young people how Myron and I met — when I came to speak for the Christian singles group to which he belonged — and how our friendship was nourished by our discoveries of all the things we had in common, beginning with faith. We both had sung in concert choirs, played instruments, and preferred classical music. We enjoyed playing baseball together. Myron is the most wonderful grower of gardens I've ever met, though my sharing in their delight involves only the passive roles of eating the produce and oohing and aahing over the flowers! More deeply, we discovered a common love of beauty in works of art and literature, in splendors of nature and architecture, in mystery. Our common goals to avoid accumulating technological gadgets (it was love at

154

first hearing when I learned that he didn't have a television set either!), to give money away, and to conserve the earth as much as possible forged deeper bonds in our friendship — bonds of common purpose and goals. Moreover, even elements of our work drew us together — Myron's comments about his experiences teaching elementary school enable me to stay better in touch with what is happening in our society concerning children, and my biblical teaching nourishes his faith. Last, but certainly not most important, we discovered that we are both very affectionate people. I especially appreciated the gentleness with which Myron expressed his care.

How can we help youth to see both the delight and the discipline of our relationships in Christ? We want them to recognize that marriage is serious business, for we are joined in a permanent union only by the purposes of God. On the other hand, we also want them to know that it is FUN. The delightful side of that dialectical tension gets lost in a puritanical understanding of Christian marriage, but the serious side gets lost in our society's view of marriage and in churches that do not recognize the higher significance of Christian marriage.

Sometimes teenagers act embarrassed or uninterested when I tell them romantic things about Myron, but it is obvious that they are secretly glad for it. They want marriage to mean more than our culture lets it mean, but they don't want it to be overbearingly purposeful.

If we want our youth to choose God's design for sexual intercourse, then we must consciously address the fact that the human body needs an escalation of pleasure. Kids understand this principle easily, for they have already learned in school that the volume of alcohol consumed or drugs taken has to continue increasing in order for the same level of "high" to be experienced. We see the effects of this principle over time in the increased violence and sexual explicitness in the media. When viewers become accustomed to a certain level of violence or sexual explicitness, more is needed to titillate.

How can we help youth understand that the same principle applies to their expressions of affection? Thus, if we believe that sexual intercourse is to be reserved for marriage, then perhaps lesser forms of intimacy should also be put on the genital sexuality side of the line, rather than the social sexuality side, and refrained from outside of marriage.

A drawing of a ladder illustrates this point. When we first see someone and are attracted, we have climbed the first rung. Other early steps include the first touch, holding hands, and the first kiss. Then the ladder moves rapidly up through steps of extended kissing, petting, heavy petting, mutual masturbation, oral sex, or other expressions of affection or lust, to the culmination of sexual intercourse. It is important when we talk with youth about the subject that we use explicit names (just as we should avoid such euphemisms as "sleeping with someone" in favor of the more truthful words *fornication* and *adultery*).

Using accurate names for what we are actually doing helps all of us to think twice about doing it. Just as with drugs and alcohol, we want to make wise decisions, for our sexual behavior is just as powerful in how it affects our future.

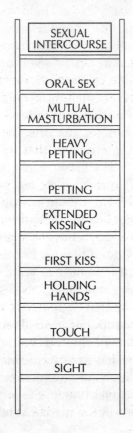

| SEXUAL INTERCOURSE |
| ORAL SEX |
| MUTUAL MASTURBATION |
| HEAVY PETTING |
| PETTING |
| EXTENDED KISSING |
| FIRST KISS |
| HOLDING HANDS |
| TOUCH |
| SIGHT |

156

While drawing this ladder and talking about it, I put a large box around "Sexual Intercourse" and tell the youth or parents that the decision to set that off as untouchable until marriage was made in my childhood. If it is set off in their decision-making process, too, because of their desire to follow the design of God, then where should they draw the line as far as which other expressions of affection might be beneficial in a relationship with another — and which expressions might be harmful and dangerous?

Because of their need in this muddled society for clear directions, youth always want me to draw the line for them. "Tell us exactly how far we can go," they often cry. I respond instead, "That is between you and the Holy Spirit."

But we cannot say, "If God is with us in all that we do, then simply imagine Jesus along with you on your date." That constant refrain in some churches seems to lead to the attitude on the part of many that God is some sort of super watchdog waiting to mark us down for bad behavior. How can we help our youth to recognize that God will give us wisdom for deciding how to express our affection, but without thereby turning God into an evil ogre trying to spoil all our fun?

A major key is helping them to realize that slavery to lusts is not fun. Desperate or frantic expressions of affection are not beautiful. God wants to come along on our dates, not to lessen the enjoyment, but to deepen it.

Perhaps one way is to challenge the youth with the adventure of finding gentle ways to express genuine affection that say more precisely because they are understated. In this outrageously gluttonous culture, it is very difficult to help people understand that more does not mean better. To engage in sexual relations near or at the top of the ladder does not mean that more love is being expressed. Some of Myron's most profound expressions of love are the simplest, such as an invitation to sit beside him on the porch swing to look at the flowers, or a light touch of my hand in a fearful moment.

157

This is a larger task than we realize, for our overscin-
tillated, overloud, overexplicit, overindulged culture has
deadened people to moments or sounds or sights or pleasures that are delicate, exquisite, gentle, skillful. How can
we recapture — for young people and for ourselves — the
wonder of understatement? How can we restore the loveli-
ness of genuine love and loving expressions of its truthfulness?

Ultimately, our goal is for all of us to find wholeness
in our relationship with God and then with each other. We
can illustrate this by drawing first a triangle to represent
the Triune God. Inside the triangle we draw a circle to
represent a person, and inside the circle we put a square,
the corners of which touch the rim of the circle, to illustrate
how our wholeness is held up by the "trampoline," which
is being supported by others. This picture shows what it
is like to be a Christian enfolded in God's love and held
up by the love of the Christian community.

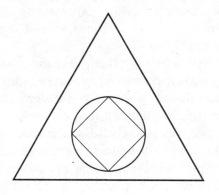

If God brings us into a marriage, it is not to make us
whole. We find our wholeness in him, and our wholeness
is supported by all kinds of people. The two circles repre-
senting marriage partners should not be drawn so that they
overlap too much, as in some marriages in which the in-

dividuality of one partner or the other is squelched. Nor should the circles be too far apart, as in many modern marriages where there is very little connection between the partners either in terms of time or in terms of common purpose. Rather, our circles overlap with a large segment of mutual interests and goals and with ample sections that prevent the unique gifts of each person from being lost. Many of the trampoline holders overlap, too, but the marriage partners' commitment to genital sexual expression only with each other enables them also to experience other deep friendships that remain chaste and social with persons of both sexes. Myron doesn't know many of my friends in other parts of the country whom I have met on speaking trips, but he has perfect confidence that all of my friendships with men and women are clearly social and not genital.

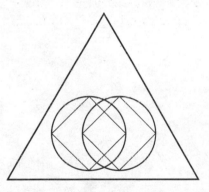

It would be impossible to draw it, but it certainly would be lovely if there were a way to illustrate the interconnections of the entire Christian community — all of us inside the triangle of God, each of us holding up many others' trampolines and being deep friends with each other, some of us committed in marriage to one other member of the community, and others choosing singleness as the best way to fulfill God's purposes in the world. How can we make such a picture attractive to teenagers and invite them into the goodness of God's design for social and genital sexuality? How can we make such a picture more of a reality in the Church?

IV *Sexual Shalom*

O let Thy sacred will
All Thy delight in me fulfill!
Let me not think an action mine own way,
But as Thy love shall sway,
Resigning up the rudder to Thy skill.

GEORGE HERBERT

The Hebrew word *Shalom* is the best term to describe the vision for human sexuality that this book intends to convey. This final section of the book presents the ideal. Previous sections have outlined questions that Christians can ask in order to move toward this vision, but here we will summarize the goals toward which we are heading as persons within the Church who are seeking God's best for their sexuality.

Shalom begins in reconciliation with God, encompasses peace with others and with ourselves, and widens out to connote such aspects of peace as health, contentment, fulfillment, satisfaction, and wholeness. Best of all, as a Hebrew professor taught me, when one person says "Shalom!" to another, he commits himself to give her whatever she might need for her wholeness that he can convey. My goal is that the Church could speak such Shalom to persons in the Christian community and in the world around us and offer the resources of biblical understanding that we all need to find sexual wholeness.

Shalom starts with the recognition that God is a gracious God. The Creator designed us for wholeness and created our sexuality to be a source of delight. That delight can best be found if we live according to our Designer's plans and purposes.

But we must admit that none of us can live perfectly according to God's best purposes for human beings. None of us is the person we would like to be. All of us have character traits we wish we didn't have. All of us are sinners in rebellion against God — and for many of us that rebellion manifests itself particularly in sexual idolatries.

However, we can rejoice in this truth of our faith: God's love and forgiveness are larger than our rebellion. Shalom for Christians is based on the assurance that in Jesus Christ we are totally forgiven and set free from our human propensity to make ourselves (and our sexual fulfillment) gods.

We also must face the fact that our culture is rife with sexual idolatry. The increasing sterility of the technological milieu makes people desperate for intimacy, and consequently many turn to genital sexuality to ease the pain of their intense loneliness. This escalates the frenzy of the search for sexual happiness, for when sexual union is taken out of the context of God's design for its protection it is eventually scarcely satisfying. Moreover, our society's overwhelming emphasis on sexual fulfillment as the most important aspect of human happiness fosters grave misunderstandings of the meaning of sexual union.

However, we can rejoice in this truth of our faith: God's grace is larger than our idolatries and misunderstandings. By the inspiration of the Holy Spirit, God's Word constantly reveals to us a better idea — the freedom of following God's design for human sexuality. We are empowered by the Holy Spirit to choose to keep sexual union within the appropriate framework of its design — as the loving sign of a permanent commitment to one person as one's partner in seeking the purposes of God.

Shalom is thus based in the character of God. For the Hebrew people, however, it was not an individualistic idea, as is so common in the modern isolated and alienated world. God's people need to recapture the biblical sense of the community, for all of us together are required to build in the Body the sexual Shalom we seek. We need the whole community to love us, to support us, to teach us, to guide us, to rebuke us, to forgive us, to bring to us God's healing. The Church must be the Church.

Shalom, based in the character of God and flourishing in the intimacy of the Christian community, enables us to be truly at peace with others and with ourselves. We will not exploit or manipulate others to gain our own sexual satisfaction, but rather will seek their wholeness. As the "trampoline" of our social sexuality is supported by the love and encouragement of other members of the Body, we will have the peace within ourselves that instills courage to resist our society's false notions of genital sexuality. We will know who we are — and the larger purposes for which we live.

We understand that God has designed sexual intercourse as the special sign of a permanent commitment between a man and a woman, a covenant that takes them beyond themselves and their own sexual pleasure into the larger realm of seeking the purposes of God's Kingdom. Christian marriage not only has God at its center but also has God as its goal. By our love and faithfulness in marriage, we model to the world the faithfulness of God, the mystery of the union of Christ and his Church.

Since sexual union carries such a holy meaning, we never want to treat it flippantly. Therefore, in the Christian community we speak of it respectfully and hold marriage in the highest esteem. Throughout the lives of members of the community, we seek to nurture the virtues necessary for sustaining both singleness and marriage according to God's purposes and a person's calling.

Shalom is a vital word for describing our vision, for living our sexuality according to God's design will lead to wholeness in many other dimensions of life. We must recognize that many contemporary social issues have arisen because our society has lost the biblical sense of sexual wholeness.

It is an enormous tragedy that so many in our culture are not finding the sexual fulfillment they so frantically seek in their endless pursuit of sexual happiness. True Shalom can only be found by living according to the design in which we were created. True Shalom is only found when we cease rebelling against God.

We who are God's people and who earnestly desire to follow the way of Jesus have great gifts to offer the world around us. We are called to be bearers of the truth about our sexuality, persons who model sexual faithfulness and the virtues of the Kingdom of God — whether we are single or married. We cannot do this alone as individuals, but together as God's people we can offer alternatives.

Perhaps most important, in the Christian community we model genuine friendship. Rooted in *agapē*, the intelligent and purposeful love that imitates the love of God and cares about the needs of others, our friendships are deeply intimate and honorable. They support single persons — both homosexual and heterosexual — and enable them to choose celibacy. The friendships of the Christian community enfold all people, so that no one feels isolated and alone in the midst of the Body.

Strong friendships with many pillars of support lead to more stable marriages in the Christian community — especially because they are founded upon a deeper understanding of how marriage demonstrates the faithfulness of God. The whole parish rejoices in each of its members and helps them to discern God's call for their singleness or marriage. Marriages are celebrated as special bonds within the community and are honored throughout the partners' lives. Young people in the Church will see the goodness of God's design as it is modeled in the relationships of permanently committed marriage partners.

Moreover, the friendships of the Christian community provide strong support for any troubled marriages in the Body. Persons of both sexes support the marriage partners in their faithfulness and offer listening ears and godly hearts to help in difficult times. The Christian community provides preventive medicine throughout the lives of its members to offset our culture's penchant for easy divorce.

The friendships in the Christian community also create an aura that welcomes children. Families are sustained, not fractured, by the activities of the parish. Children receive insight from the patterns and models of the community for discovering their own sexual identity and for delighting in God's design for their personhood. Multigenerational friendships uphold children and offer them models of the virtues needed for their future sexual wholeness. The entire Christian community assists in the nurturing of children so that their characters are formed by the revelation of God, which the Church bears.

Please remember that I am painting a picture of the ideal Christian community in this chapter. I want to offer a vision which will guide us in positive creation of sexual shalom and which will give us strength and resources to fight various sexual idolatries in our society. A sense of sexual wholeness in the Church will prevent its members from taking sexual union out of context. Consequently, the desire for abortion will be eliminated, for pregnancy will occur only within the protective framework of permanent marriage that God designed for the raising of children. Marriage partners will rejoice in the privilege of nurturing children to carry on the traditions of the faith. The community will reach out beyond itself to work for change in the structures of society that foster the escalating rate of abortions in our country.

By the time they are teenagers, the children of the community will already have gladly chosen God's design for their sexuality. They will understand that the world's notions misunderstand the true way to find sexual fulfillment. Teens will be sustained by friendships in the Body to resist the peer pressure of our culture's sexual idolatry. Instead, as God's people, they will model for their peers the better alternatives of godly sexuality.

The friendships of the Christian community will also be a source of healing and strength for those who have been broken by the lack of sexual Shalom in our world. The love of Christ at work in the members of his Body will seek to enfold and encourage homosexuals who suffer profoundly in their loneliness or confusion, victims of abuse, those who have been abandoned or rejected in divorce, children of unpeaceful homes, women who grieve an abor-

167

tion, single persons who long to be married but find no godly companions, teenagers who are overwhelmed by peer pressures, persons in troubled marriages, and any others who need the gifts of genuine friendship.

Finally, as the members of the Church display sexual Shalom, we will offer to persons outside the community our understanding of God's design and invite them into the delight of obedience. The world around us is longing for the truth and security, the delight and fulfillment of sexual Shalom.

This is a vision of what it means to be the Church living in sexual faithfulness. How can our Christian communities pursue such sexual Shalom? What does this vision mean for you as God invites you to obedience — and Joy?

WORKS CITED

Bahnsen, Greg L. *Homosexuality: A Biblical View.* Grand Rapids: Baker Book House, 1978.

Berry, Wendell, et al. "She's Come for an Abortion. What Do You Say?" *Harper's Magazine* 285, 1710 (Nov. 1992): 43-54.

Boswell, John. *Christianity, Social Tolerance, and Homosexuality.* Chicago: University of Chicago Press, 1980.

Dawn, Marva J. "The Concept of 'The Principalities and Powers' in the Works of Jacques Ellul." Ph.D. diss., University of Notre Dame, 1992.

———. "Hermeneutical Considerations for Biblical Texts" and "I Timothy 2:8-15." In *Different Voices/Shared Vision,* ed. Paul Hinlicky, pp. 15-24. Delhi, NY: American Lutheran Publicity Bureau, 1992.

———. *The Hilarity of Community: Romans 12 and How to Be the Church.* Grand Rapids: William B. Eerdmans, 1992.

———. *I'm Lonely, LORD — How Long? The Psalms for Today.* San Francisco: Harper & Row, 1983.

———. *Joy in Our Suffering: The Book of Revelation and a Theology of Weakness.* St. Louis: Concordia Publishing House, 1993.

————. *Keeping the Sabbath Wholly: Ceasing, Resting, Embracing, Feasting*. Grand Rapids: William B. Eerdmans, 1989.

Ellul, Jacques. *The Ethics of Freedom*. Trans. Geoffrey W. Bromiley. Grand Rapids: William B. Eerdmans, 1976.

————. *The Humiliation of the Word*. Trans. Joyce Main Hanks. Grand Rapids: William B. Eerdmans, 1985.

————. *Jesus and Marx: From Gospel to Ideology*. Trans. Joyce Main Hanks. Grand Rapids: William B. Eerdmans, 1988.

————. *The Meaning of the City*. Trans. Dennis Pardee. Grand Rapids: William B. Eerdmans, 1970.

————. *The New Demons*. Trans. C. Edward Hopkins. New York: Seabury Press, 1975.

————. *Propaganda: The Formation of Men's Attitudes*. Trans. Konrad Kellen and Jean Lerner. New York: Alfred A. Knopf, 1965.

————. *Reason for Being: A Meditation on Ecclesiastes*. Trans. Joyce Main Hanks. Grand Rapids: William B. Eerdmans, 1990.

————. *The Subversion of Christianity*. Trans. Geoffrey W. Bromiley. Grand Rapids: William B. Eerdmans, 1986.

————. *The Technological Bluff*. Trans. Geoffrey W. Bromiley. Grand Rapids: William B. Eerdmans, 1990.

————. *The Technological Society*. Trans. John Wilkinson. New York: Vintage Books, 1964.

————. *The Technological System*. Trans. Joachim Neugroschel. New York: Continuum Publishing Company, 1980.

————. *Violence: Reflections from a Christian Perspective*. Trans. Cecelia Gaul Kings. New York: Seabury Press, 1969.

Field, David. *The Homosexual Way — A Christian Option*. Downers Grove, IL: InterVarsity Press, 1979.

Ford, S. Dennis. *Sins of Omission: A Primer on Moral Indifference*. Minneapolis: Fortress Press, 1990.

Fortune, Marie. "How the Church Should Imitate the Navy." *The Christian Century* 109, 25 (26 Aug.–2 Sept. 1992): 765-66.

Furnish, Victor P. *The Moral Teaching of Paul*. Nashville: Abingdon Press, 1979.

Greenberg, David F. *The Construction of Homosexuality*. Chicago: University of Chicago Press, 1988.

Hauerwas, Stanley. *A Community of Character: Toward a Constructive Christian Social Ethic*. Notre Dame: University of Notre Dame Press, 1981.

Hauerwas, Stanley, and John H. Westerhoff, eds. *Schooling Christians*. Grand Rapids: William B. Eerdmans, 1992.

Hays, Richard B. "Relations Natural and Unnatural: A Response to John Boswell's Exegesis of Romans 1." *The Journal of Religious Ethics* 4, 1 (Spring 1986): 184-215.

Healy, Jane M. *Endangered Minds: Why Our Children Don't Think*. New York: Simon and Schuster, 1990.

Heddendorf, David. "A Pagan Protests Presbyterian Sex." *The Christian Century* 109, 7 (26 Feb. 1992): 213-15.

Heim, David. "Sexual Congress: The Presbyterian Debate." *The Christian Century* 108, 21 (26 June–3 July 1991): 643-44.

Huggett, Joyce. *Dating, Sex, and Friendship*. Downers Grove, IL: InterVarsity Press, 1985.

————. *Growing into Love: Before You Marry*. Downers Grove, IL: InterVarsity Press, 1982.

Jewett, Paul K. *Man as Male and Female*. Grand Rapids: William B. Eerdmans, 1975.

Joy, Donald M. *Bonding: Relationships in the Image of God*. Waco, TX: Word Books, 1985.

Kaiser, Walter C. *Toward Old Testament Ethics*. Grand Rapids: Academie Books, 1983.

Kolden, Marc. "Rollicking Advice for Evil Days: A Biblical Rationale for Christian Singing." *Word and World* 12, 3 (Summer 1992): 236-42.

Kreeft, Peter J. *Making Sense Out of Suffering*. Ann Arbor: Servant Books, 1986.

Lenski, R. C. H. *The Interpretation of St. Paul's Epistles to the Galatians, Ephesians, and Philippians*. Minneapolis: Augsburg Publishing House, 1937.

"Living Together Might Weaken Marriage Commitment." As-

171

sociated Press report. *The Columbian* (Vancouver, WA), 3 Sept. 1992.

Louw, Johannes P., and Eugene A. Nida, eds. *Greek–English Lexicon of the New Testament Based on Semantic Domains*. New York: United Bible Societies, 1988.

McNeil, John J. *The Church and the Homosexual*. Kansas City: Sheed, Andrews, and McMeel, 1976.

Nelson, C. Ellis. *Helping Teenagers Grow Morally*. Louisville: Westminster/John Knox Press, 1989.

Nelson, James B. *Embodiment: An Approach to Sexuality and Christian Thought*. Minneapolis: Augsburg Publishing House, 1978.

Paglia, Camille. "The Joy of Presbyterian Sex." *The New Republic* 205, 23 (2 Dec. 1991): 24-27.

Roberts, Steven V. "Looking for the Light in Their Souls." *U.S. News and World Report* 113, 9 (31 Aug.–7 Sept. 1992): 15.

Rosellini, Lynn. "Sexual Desire." *U.S. News and World Report* 113, 1 (6 July 1992): 60-66.

Scanzoni, Letha, and Virginia Ramey Mollenkott. *Is the Homosexual My Neighbor?* New York: Harper & Row, 1978.

Schultze, Quentin J., et al. *Dancing in the Dark: Youth, Popular Culture, and the Electronic Media*. Grand Rapids: William B. Eerdmans, 1991.

Scroggs, Robin. *The New Testament and Homosexuality*. Philadelphia: Fortress Press, 1983.

———. *Paul for a New Day*. Philadelphia: Fortress Press, 1977.

Timmerman, Joan H. *Sexuality and Spiritual Growth*. New York: Crossroad, 1992.